# Modernity and Fertility among Muslim Women in India
## With the Case Study of Uttar Pradesh

I0435695

**DR. MUDASIR AHMAD QAZI**
**&**
**DR. ATUL KUMAR YADAV**

ISBN-13: 978-1499236699
ISBN-10: 1499236697

**Modernity and Fertility among Muslim Women in India
With the Case Study of Uttar Pradesh**

**PUBLISHED BY**

CREATESPACE INDEPENDENT PUBLISHING PLATFORM

Publishing Country:
India
Date of Publishing:
25 April 2014

Designed By:
Aijaz Ahmad Bhat
Library Professional Assistant
GMC, Srinagar
Contact: salfiaijazmlis@gmail.com

## Modernity and Fertility among Muslim Women in India with the Case Study of Uttar Pradesh

***Dr. Mudasir Ahmad Qazi***
***&***
***Dr. Atul Kumar Yadav***

**To**

*Papa (Qazi Gulzar Ahmad)*
*Mamma (Mahtaba Gulzar)*
*Sister (Masarat Gul)*

WHO SACRIFICED THEIR PRESENT TO MAKE MY FUTURE BETTER . . .

# ACKNOWLEDGEMENT

I am highly thankful to my supervisor Dr. Atul Kumar Yadav for his sincere guidance and feedback. I equally thank my friend Dr. Mudasir A. Lone for bringing this book out after helping me with the editing and publishing. I must thank my friends Ashfaq Maqbool [Ph.D scholar Jamia Milia Islamia], Syed Saima [Social welfare department] and Showkat Ah. (Ph.D scholar MDU Rohtak). Thanks are also due to Dr. Sangeeta Yadav [Assistant Professor; Department of Sociology].

**Dr. Mudasir Ahmad Qazi**

# Table of Contents

# PREFACE

This book provides a modern framework of different systems-social, religious, economic and their effects on the level of fertility. It focuses on "what was", "what is" and "what is likely to be" as from the narrative of modernization in relation to fertility. An attempt has been made to analyze and review the various aspects of modernization and fertility level among Indian women. The intention has not been to present a new theory on the subject, but to explain how the growing population of India becomes an obstacle in her process of development from time to time.

It is not being claimed that there would be no omissions and shortcomings, however, an honest effort has been made to cover extensively all the major aspects of the system. It discusses different viewpoints and analyzed typologies developed by eminent scholars to make the book more comprehensive in scope. We hope that the students of sociology in general and of social demography in particular would find this book a handy and welcome contribution.

Ever since the science of demography has been developed, fertility occupies the central position in it. The growth of the population depends on fertility. It is the positive force behind the expansion as well as the dynamism of a population. Prior to the Second World War fertility was dealt with mathematically. Its dynamic character was realized only in early 1930 when the birth rates in North West Europe and North America started rising instead of declining. It was termed as the period of baby boom leading to an embarrassment to demographers. Now the role of social, psychological, cultural, economic and political factors in determining differentials of fertility was realized. It was noted that due to these factors large fluctuations occur in fertility rates. The importance of birth rate in the population growth was everywhere insisted upon. In the developing countries mortality has considerably declined with no decline of birth rate, thus leading to rapid population growth. In India during the period 1941-1951 the birth rate was 39.9% while it increased to 41.7% during the period 1951-1961 and more than 51% in the period 1981-91 and increasing so on. Fertility is basically biological though it is very much governed by the social norms. While the physiological basis of fertility is almost universal, the present day distinctions in fertility in different countries and in different regions of the same country are particularly due to social norms. The following are the factors determining fertility.

The levels and trends of fertility have been found to be low in modernized than in traditional societies. The Indian society which has been traditional for ages is transforming into modern, since independence. Many changes have been taking place in the social, occupational, and political spheres. Consequently a considerable degree of social mobility is observed in the society. The shift in the life style from traditional to modern is expected to have significant impact on the fertility behavior of the people, besides its effect on various aspects of life.

The study for the present book has been done in Shikohabad city of Firozabad district of U.P. According to District statistics Hand Book (2010:4) The old name of Shikohabad was Mohammad Mah, and Shikohabad was named after a famous emperor Dara Shikoh of the Mughal Era; the eldest brother of Aurangzeb. It is one of the tehsil headquarters of Firozabad district with a population of 107,300 (2011 census) out of which 50107 are males & 50283 females. The total number of families is 21200 in all. In which 9696 families of Muslims are residing in Shikohabad town. It is 260 kms from Delhi in East on Delhi Hawrah Railway track as well as on Delhi- Kanpur National Highway and 198 km. from Kanpur in West. It is located at 27.1° N – 78.6° E. It has an average elevation of 163 meters i.e. 534 feet. Shikohabad is a big town and a municipal board divided into 25 wards. The literacy rate is 81.68%, which is higher than the average literacy of India. It is perhaps due to availability of more educational institutions, as there are six Post Graduate Colleges in the town and many more high schools and Intermediate Collages within the limits of town. Shikohabad falls under Taj Trapezium Zone.

Different surveys have revealed different rate of fertility in different religions and castes in India. The fertility among Muslims is much more than the fertility among Hindus. Different surveys have revealed this distinction. According to the Mysore Population Study, sponsored by United Nations the fertility of different religions in Banglore city was: Hindus 5.4, Muslims 5.7 and

Christians 4.7. The average fertility in different religions in urban areas was found to be Hindus 5.2, Muslims 6.7 and Christians 5.5. This was further confirmed by the rural percentage of Hindus 4.8 and Muslims 5.0. These data were confirmed by other studies. According to the Survey of Kanpur by D.N. Majumdar, the fertility rate among Muslims and Hindus was 8.021 and 7.037 respectively. According to the study by G.B. Saxena (1969) fertility in 3 villages of Uttar Pradesh; the fertility rate among different sections of society by caste and religion was found as follows: Muslims 6.24, Hindus 6.16. Rajputs 6.77, Artisan Castes 5.50 and Bhangis and Chamars 5.43. According to S.N. Agarwal's study of fertility in 6 urbanising villages, the fertility rate among different castes was: Brahmin 7.19, Jat 7.11, Gujar and Aheer 6.97, Artisan Castes 7.16, Bhangi and Chamar 7.24. The average fertility rate for all castes was found to be 7.08. According to another study of fertility in central India; the differential fertility was as: Muslims 4.6, Hindus 4.5, Buddhists 4.9, other religions 4.1, and average for all castes 4.5.

'Education' is one of the most important social determinants of fertility because it serves the 'motivation' aspect of family limitation. Education should be of a greater importance as a determining factor with regard to reduction. Action can be taken on this front easily and in the most effective manner. We can achieve better results as far as educating the people is concerned. We can't urbanize, industrialize, raise the standard of living, break the joint family system, change the occupational structure and effectively raise the marriage age in a conceivable short period of time as easily as we can educate our people.

From social, economic, cultural, ethical, political, health & hyper-fertility point of view and immediate attention is required to arrest the galloping birth rate, which is now under a declining trend in the last decade. But still its rate of decline has to be regulated according to the economic parameters of the economy. In addition to this education to children, housing, nourishment and other facilities could only be added to the means, if the size of population is kept under reasonable limits through the effective measures of population control. The aim of family welfare is not only to limit the size of family but it includes the functions like consultation regarding age at marriage, fecundity, sex education and marital affairs; which may eradicate family troubles, tensions and difficulties. This scheme includes the programme of prohibition against the killing of female issues & carelessness during the upbringing of children. Similarly, the child care & child bearing of females having physical & mental diseases and disorders are to be given necessary importance.

Studies classifying individuals or populations on the scale of modernity confirmed an inverse association between modernity and fertility. There is a general agreement in the Indian context that Muslims have a higher fertility rate than the Hindus The data on fertility is available at community level and there is a general perception that religion plays a vital role in fertility behavior. However religious communities are not homogeneous groups. Fertility rate tends to vary across different classes within a community Hence in this research an attempt has been made to study fertility differentials among different classes within a religious community i.e. fertility differential between Muslim women who are relatively modern in terms of education arid economic well being on one hand and those who are relatively traditional on the other.

■■■■■■■■■■■■■■■■■■■■■■■■■■■■■■■■■■■■■■■■■■■■■■■■■■■■■■■■

# CHAPTER – 1
# Introduction

Drawing attention to the gravity of the population problem of India, demographer Prof. Chandrashekharan S. said that: "We are in great hurry. We cannot wait for a night. One exposure lasting five minutes leads to a baby and every year India adds one Australia to its Population".
*Hans Raj; Fundamentals of Demography (Population Studies with special reference to India); Surjeet Publications, Delhi 1978 : 319*

Most of the pre-scholars have stated that the most populationistic religion is the Islam in India. It is both because it prescribes polygamy and also encourages procreation. According to the Fatwa of Sheikh Abdullah Al-Qualquili, "Marry the affectionate prolific woman, for I shall be proud of you among the nation".[1]The ideal of marriage was procreation. It is interesting to note that Ibn-i Khaldun (1332-1406 B.C.) was of the opinion that a densely settled population helped to achieve more division of labour, more utilization of resources and ensured military and political security. He however, also pointed out that the vicious circle of population growth leads to luxurious living which in turn causes economic depression and ultimately de-population.[2] The Muslim tradition recommends marriage with four women at one time and the fifth could always be married by divorcing one of the four at short notice. Therefore, the economically well of section procreated at a high rate. The Muslim population has grown fast in almost every country including India due to Islam's encouragement to population growth.

The levels and trends of fertility have been found to be low in modernized than in traditional societies. The Indian society which has been traditional for ages is transforming into modern since independence. Many changes have been taking place in the social, occupational and political spheres. Consequently a considerable degree of social mobility is observed in the society. The shift in the life style from traditional to modern is expected to have significant impact on the fertility behaviour of the people, besides its effect on various aspects of life.

Studies classifying individuals or populations on the scale of modernity confirmed an inverse association between modernity and fertility. There is a general agreement in the Indian context that Muslims have a higher fertility rate than the Hindus. The data on fertility is available at community level and there is a general perception that religion plays a vital role in fertility behaviour. However religious communities are not homogeneous groups. Fertility rate tends to vary across different classes within a community. Hence in this research an attempt has been made to study fertility differentials among different classes within a religious community i.e. fertility differential between Muslim women who are relatively modern in terms of education and economic well-being on one hand and those who are relatively traditional on the other.

**Modernization and Fertility - The Interface:**

The questions that deserve greater research attentions are: What are the socio-economic components of women modernity? How each of them and together are related to low fertility? 'Modernization' may be defined by a variety of indices such as level of education, exposure to mass media, urban residence, type of occupation, ownership of modern household articles, degree of adherence to religious or cultural traditions. For considering the relationship between modernity and fertility the indices taken are as:

1.  Value of Children
2.  Educational Aspirations for Children
3.  Status of women
4.  Decision-making and Fertility
5.  Perception of Infant Mortality and Fertility
6.  Faith in Man's Efforts
7.  Planning Orientation
8.  Value Orientations

9.     Socio-economic status of Muslim families

The study of modernity is the key for understanding the fertility behaviour among women. Two major studies that have dealt extensively with individual modernity are: Harvard Project which was carried out in six developing countries (Smith and Inkeles 1966) and the comparative study of modernism in Brazil and Mexico (Kahl 1968). The Harvard Project was directed specifically towards the investigation of psychological aspects of modernity. A major finding of the Harvard Project is the coherence of modernity syndrome across cultures suggesting that men everywhere have the same structural mechanisms underlying their socio-psychic functioning despite the enormous variability of the culture content which they embody" (Smith and Inkeles 1966). Kahl (1968) developed a scale of values that differentiated between modern and traditional men in Brazil and Mexico. The Harvard Project and the study by Kahl are the important beginnings in the search for the 'Syndrome' of individual modernity and in the effort to link modernity to fertility change among women. Research undertaken till date shows that the Syndrome of psychological modernity includes the following traits: (1) Subjective efficacy (2) Openness to new experience and change (3) Valuation of time and punctuality (4) Acceptance of the findings of modern science and medicine (5) Granting women rights and equal treatment (6) Autonomy in the field of traditional kinship obligations and (7) Acceptance of family size limitations.

Micro level studies on modernization and fertility are few in the Indian text. A study by Mon Nag (1982) revealed that certain elements of modernization viz. education of men and women, employment of females in non-familial activity etc. are associated with low fertility, while other elements viz. declining breast feeding, improved health etc. often cause raise in fertility at least in the short run.

Analyzing Harvard Project data collected in Bihar, Pareek and Kothandapani (1969) found a significant correlation between ideal family size and birth control on one hand and some indices of modernity among women on the other. They found that education, personal modernity, political modernization, overall modernization and lack of fatalism accounted for about 10 per cent of the variance in preference for a small family among 1,300 individuals. Khan and

Parveen (1977) also observed a significant relationship between family planning adoption status and subjective efficacy as measured by the number of stories reflecting realinie coping mechanisms (RCM).Interviewing 1,865 married women in rural and urban strata of three Indian states, Biswanath Mukherjee (1979) found the three core dimensions of modernity: subjective efficacy, openness to change and propensity to plan are contributing substantially to the prediction of knowledge about the attitude towards family planning as well as favorability towards small family size. All the other micro level studies include a few questions on mass media exposure, possession of modern household articles and husband-wife communication (Mahadevan, 1979; Reddy, 1986).

Thus, even the micro level studies conducted in India had covered one or two of the dimensions of modernization among Muslim women. Further, they could not predict education and socio-economic status among different classes within the community which will have a direct influence on the variance in total fertility. Also the effect of achievement motivation on fertility behaviour due to modernization has not been examined. Hence, it is proposed to examine in greater detail the *"Effect of modernity on fertility among Muslim women"*. The findings of the present study would be of immense value for promoting small family norm through appropriate communication strategies aimed at manipulating women fertility behaviour. In a committee which is perceived to be less receptive of the efficacies of small family norm.

Theories of Population: Malthian and Neo-Malthian- A Central Theme:

Malthus started his Essay by laying down two postulates: "First, that food is necessary to the existence of man." "Secondly, the passion between the sexes is necessary and will remain nearly in its present state."[3] He argued that the power of population is definitely greater than the power in the earth to produce subsistence for men. Population, when unchecked increases in a geometrical ratio. Subsistence increases only in an arithmetical ratio. A slight acquaintance with numbers will show the immensity of the first power in comparison with the second."[4] The following propositions were put forth by Malthus, to establish his theory: "(1) Population is necessarily limited by the means of subsistence; (2) Population invariably increases where the means of subsistence increase unless prevented by some very powerful and obvious checks; (3) These checks, and the checks which repress the superior power of population and its effects on a level with the means of subsistence, are all resolvable into moral restraint, vice and misery."[5] Malthus recognized that the growth of population does not go unchecked. Pointing out powerful checks on the growth of population, he said, "The first of these checks may, with property, be called the preventive check to population, and the absolute necessity of their operation in the case supposed is as certain and obvious as that man cannot live without food."[6]

According to E.P. Hutchinson the idea of arithmetical ratio concerning the growth of the means of subsistence was unanimously rejected by scholars. As a general rule the following points were raised as criticisms against Malthusian theory:

1.     As has been already pointed out, the ratio of arithmetical progression of means of subsistence and the geometrical progression of population growth was never proved.
2.     In so many cases the theory of the growth of the means of subsistence in arithmetical ratio was not proved.
3.     Malthus did not clearly distinguish between fecundity and fertility or the physiological capacity to reproduce and the actual reproductive performance.
4.     The classification of checks on population growth as preventive and positive were cited as an example of poor classification, since they were not independent categories.
5.     Malthus did not succeed in connecting positive and preventive checks with his theory.
6.     Malthus placed undue emphasis on the limitation of the supply of land. Agricultural production tremendously increased through agricultural revolution in the 19th century.
7.     Malthus painted a gloomy picture of the future growth of population. According to Ralph Thomlinson, his predictions did not come out to be true due to agricultural revolution.[7]
8.     One finds a contradiction in the twin role of Malthus as a scientist and as a moralist. His role as a scientist was vitiated by his attempts of opposing birth control.
9.     He favoured postponement of marriage and even total abstinence.

In spite of the above mentioned criticisms, Kingsley Davis has rightly maintained that though not empirically valid Malthusian theory was theoretically significant. His name occupies an important place in the history of population thought.[8] He was the first thinker who systematically and thoroughly applied inductive method to social science.

Neo-Malthusianism:

Neo-Malthusians are the successors of Malthus. They were keen supporters of family planning movement. According to them Malthus was the first thinker who established that uncontrolled increase of population will lead to poverty and therefore birth control must be popularized. Among the most important neo-Malthusian thinkers may be mentioned Mary Stopes of Great Britain and Margaret Senger of U.S.A., besides so many supporters in Western Europe. These people popularized chemical and mechanical methods of birth control. The family planning movement gradually extended not only to the entire Western World but also to the countries of Asia and Africa continents.

According to Neo-Malthusianism, Malthus did not distinguish between sex desire and desire for children. Both these are fulfilled by the same physical organs. The sex desire also involves desire for reproduction. Neo-Malthusians however, do not accept this view. They reject the Malthusian theory that sex desire is identical with the desire for children. According to them sex desire is a natural and biological desire. It is the most powerful physical and psychological desire among the adults. Its repression leads to so many mental and physical evils. Desire for children, on the other hand, particularly depends upon social, moral and cultural values. It is not inherent but a product of socio-economic conditions. Fulfillment of sex desire is must for normal and healthy life. The desire for children however, should be adjusted according to favorable or unfavorable circumstances. Only that woman should reproduce who is physically and mentally fit for the purpose. Males and females should be allowed to satisfy their sex desire without procreation. There is no moral evil in using chemical or mechanical means of birth control to satisfy sex desire.

Neo-Malthusians acclaimed Malthus as their leader in family planning movement. However, the French economists did not agree with this idea. They pointed out that Malthus would have called modern means of birth control, "Unmitigated conjugal fraud". He would have declared them as antichristian and ungodly. In his essay on population Malthus has pointed out that artificial means of birth control are much inferior as compared to natural restrictions such as self-control. The Neo-Malthusians, on the other hand, maintain that in the second edition of his essay, Malthus concluded that population cannot be controlled by moral restraint alone. Moral restraint is a means which cannot be expected to be practiced by ordinary people. Therefore in spite of himself Malthus was prepared to allow artificial means of birth control. The Neo-Malthusians have advanced the following arguments in favour of their artificial birth control movement:

1.      Birth control is necessary to limit the family size in the context of available economic means; otherwise the standard of living will fall down considerably. Without limiting the family, it is impossible to bring up children properly and pay attention to their physical, mental and moral development.

2.      Birth control is equally necessary to limit the burden on world economy. This has already reached its saturation point. Therefore, it has no more capacity to feed the additional growing number of world population.

3.      Birth control is necessary on the ground of health and medical care as well.

4.      Those who oppose the Neo-Malthusian approach maintained that birth control is unnatural.

5.      Another argument advanced against birth control is that it is immoral. To this Neo-Malthusians point out that morality is a relative concept.

The terms and concepts used in the study:

Modernization involves changes not only in the material culture of society but also in its belief system, values and the way of life on the whole. It is a process of the transformation of a society from its backward outlook to a forward-looking, progressive and prosperous structural build-up, but modernity is the state of change in the attitudes, while modernization is the process of change.

'Modernity has been defined by a variety of indices, such as level of education, exposure to mass media, urban residence, type of occupation, ownership of modern household items or degree of adherence to religious or cultural traditions. When individuals or populations are classified on a scale of modernity, an inverse relationship between modernity and fertility is found (Fawcett, 1970).

From the Harvard Project, Smith and Inkeles (1966) assumed that "modernity would emerge as a complex but coherent set of psychic dispositions manifested in general qualities such as a sense of efficacy, readiness for new experience and interest in planning, linked in turn, to certain dispositions to act in institutional relations as in being in active citizen, valuing science, maintaining one's autonomy in kinship matters and accepting birth control".

Prof. Williamson (1969) from the Harvard Project data concluded that subjective efficacy and ideal family size function more as independent determinants than as intervening variables. It is one of the most important studies yet undertaken to clarify the linkages via, both social and psychological routes between modernity and fertility. KahI (1968) conducted another cross-national study on modernism", which is similar to the Harvard Project in its conceptual and methodological approach. He developed a scale of values that differentiated between modern and traditional men in Brazil and Mexico. A consistent inverse relationship between degree of modernism and size of ideal family was shown for most occupational groups, but only a few of the differences were statistically significant. The cross-cultural work of McClelland on the achievement motive is another attempt to understand an aspect of modernity among women (McClelland1961, Mc Clelland and Winter 1969).

Modernity has also been found to be related to birth limitation. The study of Korean family planning behaviour by Chung, Palmore and Lee (1972) showed a sensitive relationship of modern attitudes to contraceptive practice. A study by Coombs and Freedman (1979) examined some of the connecting links between modernization in a developing society, particularly urbanization, increased education for women and preferences for a desired number of children. Following Smith and Inkeles, Fawcett and Bomstein (1973) presented three themes of modernization reflected in personality orientation which are considered particularly relevant to family planning and fertility change, subjective efficacy, orientation towards time and openness to change. Many studies supported a negative relationship between fertility and an advanced level of modernization as a social variable (Fawcett and Bomstein, 1973; Ryder, 1959; United Nations, 1953; Adelman and Morris, 1966). Kahl (1968) reported that the family system in Rio de Janeiro appears to be more modern than the family system in Mexico City and this, he claims, accounts for the wider difference between provincial and metropolitan fertility norms in Brazil compared to Mexico.

Both the Indianapolis study (Kiser and Whelpton, 1953; Kiser, 1962) and Princeton study (Westoff et al. 1961; Westoff, et al., 1963) have attempted to show how differences in family structure produce differential fertility.

**Openness to Change:**

Openness to change refers to the readiness for new experience and openness to innovation and change, (Inkeles, 1966). In the present study openness to change will be measured by a set of five statements relating to opinion on (1) working of married women in the midst of men (2) medical termination of pregnancy (3) remarriage of young widows (4) involvement of women in decision making and (5) adoption of innovations. All the statements except acceptance of innovations (dichotomous) will have five alternative responses. A score of 1 will be given for strong disapproval and 5 for 'strong approval'. With regard to opinion on adoption of innovations a score of 1 will be assigned for 'disapproval' and 2 for approval' Thus the index on openness to change will have a minimum score of 5 and a maximum of 22.

**Faith in man's efforts:**

It refers to the belief that men can exert control over his environment (Kluckhohn and Strodbeck, 1961). Several studies of modernism obtained measures of people's beliefs about their personal capacity to control what appears to them as observe of how much they feel controlled by luck, supernatural beings and the like (Kahl, 1968; Rogers, 1969). Here, this dimension will be measured on the basis Of responses to six statements, each with three alternatives. An index will he developed giving a score of 1 to responses reflecting submissiveness to nature, 2 for don't know and 3 for" responses indicating mastery over nature. The low score (6-11) will be indicate submissiveness to nature while high score (16-18) will show mastery over nature.

**Planning Orientation:**

According to Prof. KahI (1968) planning orientation refers to making plans in advance for the important events and phases of life. The same definition will be adopted here Planning orientation will be measured by asking six statements relating to advance planning of family size, education and welfare of children and their own future. All the statements except one (dichotomous) have three alternative responses. An index will be developed based on responses to these statements assigning a score of 1 for 'no planning', 2 for "don't know' and 3 for 'advance planning and in case of dichotomous statement 1 for 'no planning' and 2 for 'advance planning'. Thus, the low score, (6-8) will indicate poor planning while high score (16-47) will show advance planning.

**Aspiration for Education of Children:**

Aspiration is defined as "a desired future state of being" (Rogers, 1969) Here, the aspiration for education of children refers to the degree of parental aspiration in providing college education to their children. It will be measured by asking the respondents to state the highest level of education they would like to provide to their children even in times of financial crisis.

**Decision-making in Family Matters:**

Decision-making refers to persons making crucial decisions on matters affecting the welfare of the family members. It is likely to differentiate the more modern from the less modern as the former is more likely to make decision in consultation with their spouses, while the latter make decisions mostly by themselves. For measuring decision making in the family, the respondents will be asked to state as to, who, in the family would decide (1) the timing of birth of first child (2) family size (3) spacing of children and (4) contraceptive use. An index will be developed assigning score 1 for 'no decision', 2 for 'elders alone', 3 for 'husband/wife alone' and 4 for 'husband and wife jointly'. Thus, the minimum score on decision-making will be 4 while the maximum will be 16.

**Status of women:**

Status literally means position in relation to other. The United Nations viewed status of women in terms of actual control on their lives. According to United Nations (1975) the status of woman in society can be determined by her composite status which can be ascertained from the extent of control that she has over her own life derived from access to knowledge, economic resources and the degree of autonomy enjoyed in the process of decision making and choice at crucial points in her life cycle. In an international comparative study on women's rights and fertility (Dixon, 1978), the status of women was measured by the number of years of schooling, their integration in major areas of political decision making and their age at marriage. In the present study status of women will refer to economic and social freedom enjoyed by the women in the family. It will be measured by asking nine statements to respondent wives relating to owning of property, maintaining bank account, freedom to argue in case of difference of opinion and joint decision-making on crucial matters such as family size, contraceptive use, etc. An index will be developed giving a score of 1 or 2 for 'sometimes' and 3 for 'yes'. Thus, the minimum score will be 9 and the maximum 27. The low score (9-14) will indicate low status of women while high score (22-27) will show high status.

**Fertility:**

According to United Nations, "Natural fertility is the fertility which exists in the absence of deliberate birth control".[9] According to the same source controlled fertility is the fertility which involves a deliberate use of birth control.[10] The term birth control is used in a broad sense to include intentional abortions, sterilization and complete abstinence from coitus.[11] In this connection it is necessary to differentiate between fertility and fecundity. Fertility "refers to the actual reproductive performance applied to an individual or a group."[12] On the other hand, fecundity refers to "the capacity of a man, a woman, or a couple to participate in reproduction (i.e. the reproduction of a live child)."[13] Fertility can be measured through birth rate. Fecundity however cannot be measured. A man or a woman who has given birth to a live child is considered fertile. The total number of children born by one couple is known as Family size. The sequence of births of children is Birth order. This sequence in the case of mothers is known as Parity which is decided by the number of children born alive. The biological limits of child birth are known as Reproductive span. The physiological limits of child bearing capacity and period are known as Theoretical maximum fertility. Abortions and still births are classified as Reproductive wastage. Birth control by self- control is known as Voluntary abstinence.

In the words of demographer Lewis and Thompson, 'Fertility is generally used to indicate the actual reproductive performance of a woman or groups of women. The Crude Birth Rate (number of Births per 1000 population per year) is only one measure of fertility.

**Fecundity:**

Fecundity refers to the number of children an average woman is capable of bearing. Such factors as health, finances and personal decision sharply affect fecundity.

**Crude birth rate:**

CBR is the number of live births for every thousand people in a population. We can calculate this rate by dividing the number of live births in a year by the total population and then multiplying the result by 1,000.

**Mortality and Expectancy:**

Mortality or the number of deaths in a society's population also influences population size similar to the crude birth rate. We can calculate the crude death rate or the number of deaths annually per 1,000 people in the population. Crude death rate can be obtained by dividing the number of deaths in a year by the total population and then multiplying the result by 1,000.

**Infant mortality rate:**

Infant mortality rate is the number of deaths among infants under age one for each 1,000 live births in a year.

A low infant mortality correlates with a higher life expectancy which is the average lifespan of a society's population.

## Formulae Used Under the Study:

(1) Child Women Ratio (CWR) =

$$\text{CWR} = \frac{\text{Children of the age of less than 5 years}}{\text{Women of Reproduction Age Group (15-49)}} \times 1000$$

(2) Crude Birth Rate (CBR) =

$$\text{CBR} = \frac{\text{Total no. of children who took Birth in a year}}{\text{Mid-year Total population}} \times 1000$$

(3) General Fertility Rate (GFR) =

$$\text{GFR} = \frac{\text{Number of live births during a year}}{\text{Mid-year population of women between the age of 15-49 yrs.}} \times 1000$$

(4) Age specific Fertility Rate (ASFR) =

$$\text{ASFR} = \sum_{15}^{49} \frac{\text{Specific age group of woman}}{\text{Mid-year population of women of the ages of 15-49 yrs.}} \times 1000$$

(Prof. Bogue has said that 'ASFR' is the number of births per year to 1000 women of a particular age i.e. 15-44 or 49.)

(5) Total Fertility Rate (TFR) =

$$\text{TFR} = \sum_{15}^{49} \frac{\text{No. of live births during the year}}{\text{Mid-year population of women of 15-49 age groups}} \times 1000$$

## Historical Background:

Ever since the science of demography has been developed, fertility occupies the central position in it. The growth of the population depends on fertility. It is the positive force behind the expansion as well as the dynamism of a population. Prior to the Second World War fertility was dealt with mathematically. Its dynamic character was realized only in early 1930 when the birth rates in North West Europe and North America started rising instead of declining. It was termed as the period of baby boom leading to an embarrassment to demographers. Now the role of social, psychological, cultural, economic and political factors in determining differentials of fertility was realized. It was noted that due to these factors large fluctuations occur in fertility rates. The importance of birth rate in the population growth was everywhere insisted upon. In the developing countries mortality has considerably declined with no decline of birth rate, thus leading to rapid population growth. In India during the period 1941-1951 the birth rate was 39.9% while it increased to 41.7% during the period 1951-1961 and more than 51% in the period 1981-91 and increasing so on.

## Nature of Fertility:

As has been already pointed out, fertility is basically biological, though it is very much governed by the social norms, while the physiological basis of fertility is almost universal. The present day distinctions in fertility in different countries and in different regions of the same country are particularly due to social norms. The following are the factors determining fertility.

**Social and Cultural Determinants:**

Demographers Kingsley Davis and Judith Blake[14] have developed a model classifying the intermediate variables through which social factors affect the stages of child bearing. This model is as follows:

**Factors Affecting Exposure to Intercourse (Intercourse Variables):**

(A)    Those governing the formation and dissolution of unions in the reproductive period.

    1.    Age of entry into sexual unions.

    2.    Permanent celibacy: Proportion of women never having sexual union.

    3.    Part of the reproductive period spent after or between unions:

        (a) When unions are broken by divorce, separation or desertion.

        (b) When unions are broken by death of husband.

(B)    **Factors governing exposure to intercourse within unions:**

    4.    Voluntary abstinence.

    5.    Involuntary abstinence (from impotence, illness, unavoidable but temporary separations).

    6.    Coital frequency (excluding periods of abstinence).

**Factors Affecting Exposure to Conception (Conception Variables):**

    7.    Fecundity affected by involuntary causes.

    8.    Use of contraception.

        (a) By mechanical or chemical means.

        (b) By other means.

    9.    Fecundity or infecundity as affected by voluntary causes (Sterilization, sub-incision, medical treatment etc.)

**Prof. Srivastav B.K.[15] (2007)** in his study has shown the causes which are usually responsible for high fertility rate may be observed as:

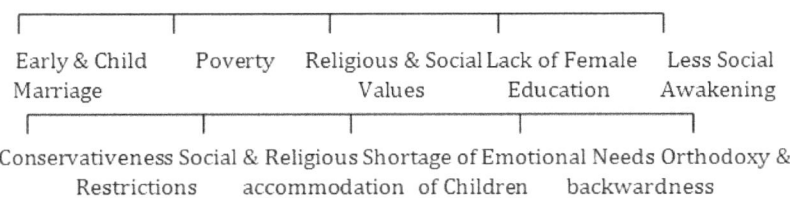

| Early & Child Marriage | Poverty | Religious & Social Values | Lack of Female Education | Less Social Awakening |
|---|---|---|---|---|
| Conservativeness | Social & Religious Restrictions | Shortage of accommodation | Emotional Needs of Children | Orthodoxy & backwardness |

Demographer **Chahar K.S.**[16] **(1990)** has also briefly discussed the Social, Religious and Economic factors and causes responsible for high fertility rate, to be given as:

**(a)** **Social Determinants of Fertility:** These factors are responsible both for high as well as low fertility in every society. Among the social factors, mention may be made particularly of the following:

    (1) Whether society respects both the sexes and only one sex i.e. either women or men?

    (2) Whether it is socially believed that small size of the family is a blessing or a curse?

    (3) Whether family planning devices are socially a welcome or these are opposed and hated?

    (4) Whether woman is considered a co-partner in family affairs or her consent is essential before she is loaded with responsibilities of motherhood or whether she is considered only a method for satisfying the lust of men?

    (5) Whether the women are educated or illiterate?

    (6) How far the women are socially allowed to decide family affairs?

    (7) How far has the society been in a position to provide facilities like those of schooling, health, employment etc.?

    (8) How far the society recognizes that it is responsible for proper bringing up of the children?

    (9) Whether society prefers single or joint family system and if so by and large which pattern is it following?

    (10) Whether marriage is considered only a friendship or a permanent alliance to be dissolved by God?

    (11) The age at which the society will like the boys and girls to marry.

    (12) What is divorced rate in the society?

(13)    Whether the society encourages widow re-marriage or not?

(14)    What is the climate of the country; there by what is the age of the girl at which she becomes capable of producing children?

(b)    **Religious Determinants of Fertility:** Like social determinants, there are religious determinants of fertility as well. Some such factors are:

(1)    How far religion dominates the society?

(2)    What is the attitude of religious leaders towards family planning?

(3)    How far religion and religious leaders are under the influence of politicians and political leaders?

(4)    Does the religion opposes the family planning system or simply adopts a neutral attitude?

(c)    **Economic Determinants of Fertility:** Economic determinants weigh considerably so far as fertility is concerned. Some of the important determinants are:

(1)    What is the living standard of the people and what living standard does the society wish to maintain?

(2)    Whether the country is overpopulated or the society wants to have manpower to improve economic lot of the people?

(3)    Whether the population is contented due to religious or other factors; what are its present economic conditions?

(4)    What are the chances of employment for the growing population?

(5)    Whether each child is considered a source of income or economic burden on the parents?

(6)    Whether economically the parents, by and large can bear the expenses involved in the development and brining up of the children?

(7)    What is the economy of the society?

(8)    Whether in economy; the women are earning partners along with men or not?

(9)    Whether economically the people can afford to have sources of recreation and/or for them women is the only source of recreation?

## Future of Fertility in India[17]:

The future growth in India's population will be largely determined by the trend in birth rate which unfortunately goes on quite high in spite of all efforts in the family planning movement. Undoubtedly, the movement has made some headway, but in the context of the total country and its rate of fertility the progress is not significant. This is confirmed by the census data of 1981, 1991 and 2001 respectively. The main hurdles in the way of control are conservativeness, illiteracy, communalism, lower economic status and lack of sufficient efforts and co-ordination.

## Population Policy in India:

Demographer Hyrdal has said that, "A population policy can be nothing less than a social policy at large". But in defining population policy Prof. Berelson (1972) has outlined the following three main characteristics: (1) It includes the action taken by government in the form of a statement of position, laws, decrees or administrative programs. (2) It covers population events.(3) It refers to both the intentions and consequences designed to alter population events. In this way population policy is characterized by the three components of population change viz. fertility, mortality and migration. Thus a population policy of a country refers to the governmental measures with reference to population change. It covers (i) Policies Influencing Mortality i.e. aim of reduce of mortality rate, through the concept of public health. The W.H.O.[18]has defined health as "A state of complete physical, mental and social well-being and not merely the absence of disease or infirmity (ii) Policies Influencing Migration (iii) Population Policies Influencing Fertility. These may be classified as (1) anti-natalist (a) to accept existing values and attitudes and diminish the economic liability of having children (b) To modify the norms by glorifying values concerning reproduction. This includes such legal measures as lowering the minimum age for marriage and reinstating the old custom of divorce on the basis of infertility (c) To relax the taboos on illegitimacy (2) Anti-natalist policies i.e. limiting the growth of population. This policy includes provisions of contraceptive services, liberalization of abortion laws and rising age at marriage.

(A)     **Provision of Contraceptive Services:** One finds both optimistic and pessimistic approaches towards the population check by provision of contraceptive services.

Arguments are available on both the sides. Therefore, it has been concluded by Prof. Kingsley Davis, "The need is not to abandon the family planning programs; but to put equal or greater resources into other approaches."[19] However, it is undeniable that today family planning programs are getting whole hearted support everywhere. It has been accepted as a basic human right those persons can decide the number and spacing of their children."We believe that the objective of family planning is the enrichment of human life; not its restrictions, that family planning by assuring greater opportunity to each person, free man to attain his individual dignity and reach high full potential."[20]

(B)     **Liberalization of Abortion Laws.**
(C)     **Raising Age at Marriage.**
(D)     **Incentives:** Direct or indirect incentives in cash or in kind that are given to an individual, couple or group in order to encourage some over behavioural change may be immediate or deferred.[21]
(E)     **Social and Economic Development.**
(F)     **Nutrition and health services for mothers and children.**
(G)     **Social Security.**
(H)     **Population education in the syllabi of school education and out of school youths.**

In our country 'Family Planning Programme' drew the attention of the population and was felt that main reason of Indian poverty is its growing population. The population is rapidly increasing in the comparison of food and if this growth rate is not checked then the problem could be serious to any extent. Prof. A.G. Kaul rather rightly said that, "A reduction in fertility would make the process of modernization a success."[22]

Keeping in view the magnitude of the population problems the demographers, researchers, economists and social reformers, all raised their voice in favour of the implementation of family planning programmes, which is the need of today in India.

## FACTORS AFFECTING BIRTH RATE AND FERTILITY

In vast majority of cases both the men and the women have fertility and capacity to produce children. There are however many factors which affect and influence fertility. In the past years, there was no check or control in so far as child producing was concerned. But today the fertility is being checked in the sense that most of the people in the urban areas or the elite sections of the society wish to have very limited family. They are following family planning devices or with the help of or means including abortion, checking the size of the family. A family of three children is today considered a normal family, though some people still like a smaller family. There are people also who do not at all like to have a child, though they are leading a married life and have capacity to produce children. In fact whole programme of limiting the size of the family has become more necessary from social point of view rather than any other viewpoint. Some of the important factors which effect fertility may be discussed as under:

**(A)Biological Factors:** In fertility biological factors play a very leading role. In biological factors most important is the health and related factors are diseases, food habits etc. As the health conditions and standards go on improving with that fecundity will also increase and death rate will come down.

**(B)Indirect Social Factors:** These are the factors which are influenced by social customs and in turn affect fertility. Normally however, the people do not consider these factors which influence fertility. On the other hand these are treated as social values. Usually these factors instead of directly influencing fertility indirectly influence them. Important factors being (i) Age at Marriage   (ii) Polygamy (iii) Separation and Divorce (iv) Widowhood (v) Post-Partum Abstinence(vi) Abstinence and Menstruation (vii) Celibacy and (viii) Frequency of coitus.

**(i)**     **Age at Marriage:** It appears that fertility goes down when marriage takes place at a late stage. It is a well-known fact that fertility rate is higher where marriages take place at comparatively early ages, as compared with the people who marry at late stage. In India marriages take place at very young age. Thus it is not universally correct that fertility will be low, if the marriages take place at late stage. Since in India in spite of the fact that marriages take place at young age but sexual relationship is socially permitted when the girl has reached puberty, therefore early marriage does not influence fertility. Another fact which ought to be borne in mind is that in birth matters social and cultural conditions play a very big role. Cultural conditions and social customs directly influence biological needs and their satisfaction. These also influence age at marriage, child birth, age etc. and thus importance and significance can in no way be under estimated.

(ii)     **Polygamy:** Another indirect social factor which influences fertility is polygamy. It is a system under which a husband can have more than one wife. This system is not very popular these days. If Polygamy is compared with a system where the husband has only one wife, then there is possibility that fertility per woman may be very less. But the facts have not supported this belief. When a husband begins to maintain more than one wife, then his first wife get more opportunities of meeting the husband and thus produce children as compared with the other wives, who are married at late stage and due to old age of the husband the sexual meetings between the husband and the wife are very less. As such, chances of such wives producing children are considerably reduced. Since the husband himself is old and the wife is not permitted to have sexual exposures with other young man, the result is that birth of children considerably goes down.

(iii)     **Separation and Divorce:** It is not certain that after marriage, both the husband and the wife will always have cordial relations. There can be and usually are unhealthy and strained relations as well, which result either in separation or divorce. But divorce or separation always does not mean low fertility. It is related to many factors e.g. how frequent is the separation, what is separation period, the age of the children when the parents opt for separation, age of the parents themselves at the time of separation or divorce, the interval between the separation and remarriage.

(iv)     **Widowhood:** Widowhood quite obviously influences fertility. It is because without her husband she cannot have legal children. But the effect of widowhood on fertility depends on how soon she decides to remarry. If a widow decides to remarry immediately, fertility will not be affected, but if she decides to remarry at a very late stage or not to remarry at all, obviously fertility will be affected. Whether widow remarriage system is good or bad or it should or should not be encouraged very much depends on social conditions and attitude of the people differs. In India for a long time widow remarriage was discouraged, though the situation has changed now.

(v) **Post-Partum Abstinence:** Fertility is also affected by the restrictions imposed by the society or otherwise on reunion or sexual exposure of the husband and wife, after the birth of a child. Obviously when this period is long fertility will be less, when the period is short, the husband and wife will get opportunity to meet and chances of fertility are bright and more.

(vi) **Abstinence and Menstruation:** Almost it is accepted that the husband and wife should remain separate from each other, during menstruation period of the wife. In some societies it is very strictly observed and the women during menstruation period are not permitted to attend many social functions and religious ceremonies, while in other societies, this practice is not observed with great rigidity. Since the period of menstruation is practically that of separation, therefore, fertility is affected.

(vii) **Celibacy:** Fertility is also affected and influenced by social and self- imposed controls about marriages. In many societies including our society, it is believed that ideal age of marriage was 25 years for the boy and 20 years for the girl i.e. up to this age the boy should not marry. Similarly there are legal provisions about the marriageable age of the boys and girls in India. Thus when self or socially imposed restrictions are effective, fertility is bound to be effected, because during the period of such a control the boy and girl will have no opportunity to meet and thus no children will be produced.

(viii) **Frequency of Coitus:** What is the frequency of coitus is an influencing factor in fertility. It is very difficult to find out and assess how frequently the husband and the wife meet together, but usually it is believed that such meetings should be less frequent because more frequent meetings adversely affect health. But one interesting fact which has been noticed is that whereas in India husband and wife meet less frequently.

(C)**Direct Factors Affecting Fertility:** Along with indirect factors there are direct factors as well which affect fertility. These include use of contraceptives, oral pills, other artificial measures, abortions, infanticide etc. All these factors are so important that these need careful study. In every society, these days there is a tendency that family size should be small and population exposition should be checked, otherwise many economic, social and political problems are bound to arise. Thus the most important direct factor which effects fertility is family planning drive in every society. There are different methods for achieving this objective and each objective obviously effects fertility. Today there is no advanced country of the world which is not interested in checking fertility. Every attempt is made to educate as well as to convince the people about checking fertility. Some such methods which are used now these days, are as follows:

(i) **Oral Pills:** It is believed that a fertile woman, if she uses these pills for 20 days in a month, the chances of pregnancy is reduced to the minimum. In some cases when these are used without medical advice there can be complications, but use with medical advice can solve many such problems as headache, fatness etc. which such tablets can create. Since the pills have been found most effective against pregnancy, these are in common use in USA. Thus the use of these pills checks fertility.

(ii) **Loop:** It is another device for checking fertility. It is used by women and the success of avoiding the birth of children is about 96%. Loop can be removed at any time. It is most useful in checking period of birth between the two children. In India when it was introduced in 1970, it was quite popular, but subsequently due to many complications the women avoided using it. But the use of loop very effectively checks fertility.

(iii) **Condom:** It is used by men and is the easiest way of checking the fertility and child birth. It can be used without the help of any doctor. In India, it is being supplied to the married couples at very concessional rates. These are now being commonly used and providing very useful method for controlling family size. In addition to this there are many other artificial methods for checking population growth and fertility. These end in getting the wife operated so that she is not in a position to produce children.

(iv) **Abortion:** Quite frequently it is observed that a woman becomes pregnant at a time when she does not wish to have any child. In many societies it is quite permissible that she should be allowed to have abortion, though in many societies it is not so allowed. How far abortions influence fertility is difficult to assess because in many cases the people are not willing to supply information due to legal or social problems and in many other cases it is difficult to distinguish between voluntarily abortion and miscarriage. Whether abortion should legally be allowed or not, is a problem on which opinions can differ, but the fact remains that today in many advanced societies of the world, there is no hesitation in following it and as such it is a method which is used for checking fertility and it influences and effects birth rates of the children.

(v) **Infanticide:** Another factor which directly effects fertility is the practice of infanticide. It is a practice which was quite well followed in illiterate persons in the past. In some societies children who are blind, handicapped or those who are born at ill time etc. are killed from there very birth and so is the notion about the child born at the time of whose birth some death takes place. In poor society the children are killed because there is shortage of food. Balikci, Firth and Fei in their studies have also come to the conclusion that food shortage is responsible for infanticide in many societies. Even in such societies daughters are killed because they cannot go for hunting or are not economically self-sufficient. Not only this, but when they grow up even then much is to be spent on their marriage and dowry. In such societies obviously the ratio of men is always higher as compared with those of the women. In such societies where the girls are killed the attitude adopted is that the work of the women is merely to plait mats and fill the water bottles and when one or two girls have born that should be enough. But men are needed because they go out for catching the fish and doing other work. Prof. Lang in his study carried out in 1946 came to the conclusion that "Female infants may not be killed outright but in families where food is short sons are better fed. Everywhere girls do not actually starve, epidemics will be much likely to carry them off than their better nourished brothers."

From the study of all factors which directly or indirectly affect fertility, it will be seen that some are really effective, whereas others only very marginally affect birth rate or fertility. In the words of Harrison and Boyce, "The brief survey of direct and indirect factors affecting fertility has shown that for the vast majority of societies there are few social mechanisms for controlling fertility and except in a very few societies that do not appear to be very effective. The fact is that in most societies people do not wish to restrict fertility but on the contrary, they desire to produce the maximum number of children." It is however difficult to agree with the learned authors that even today the people are not interested in restricting fertility or are in any way interested in having maximum number of children. Today in many societies the people are quite keen to have limited families and are adopting many measures to check fertility.

**(D)Other Social Factors:** The researcher has discussed some direct and indirect factors which affect fertility. There are other social factors as well which affect fertility. Some such important factors are:

(i)     **Food Supply:** It is usually believed that in societies where there is shortage of food supply there is less fertility. Malthus in his theory for the first time, tried to establish that nature maintains a balance between food supplied and growth of population and that there is a link between the two. But it is difficult to logically and scientifically establish this relationship in actual practice. In fact it is difficult to link that shortage of food supplies checks fertility in a society. Prof. Wynne and Edwards are of the view that in non-human animal society's growth rate is much higher than food supplies, but still animals are not seen dying of starvation. They are of the opinion that what is true of animal society, should be true of human society as well. Stop in a study conducted in 1962 has also supported the viewpoint of Wynne and Edwards. Prof. Douglas has however not contributed to this viewpoint, because unlike animal population human population is affected by shortage of food supplies but by local customs, social prestige etc. it however, cannot be denied that food supplies if not directly affects to a considerable extent but indirectly checks fertility. We know that in many countries where there is shortage of food supplies, the young couples are advised to restrict family size so that it becomes easy to solve food problem of the country.

(ii) **Economic Conditions:** Then another factor which effects fertility is the economic conditions of the people. Economic conditions are directly linked with fertility. Usually in agricultural 'zamindar families' fertility is very high because they follow joint family system and husband and wife always live together. Moreover agriculturists so much produce for them that everyone is economically sound. It is the reason that in the village's fertility is very high, particularly among the zamindars. On the other hand in the cities the people are mostly salaried ones and they have their own limitations. They have shortage of accommodation and with their limited income they find it difficult to bear the expenses of bringing up the children. It is the primary reason that among salaried people an attempt is made to keep the fertility low. The people in the urban areas think in terms of giving higher education to the children, providing them high living standard and more facilities and amenities of life and as such they do not like to have more children. Prof. Harrison and Boyce say, "The very poor in industrial societies can often see no advantage a handicap than nine.... If a man does not have dependents on whom will he depend when he is old and ill?"

(iii) **Family System:** Family system also effects fertility. In a joint family system where the elders always have an eye on the activities of the youngsters and accommodation is short, the chances of husband and wife meeting together are reduced to considerable extent. Hence fertility is low. On the other hand where there is single family system and the couple lives alone, both have ample opportunities with the result that fertility goes up. But now these days it is not exactly the case. Usually the husband and wife both are employed and they have no elder lady at home to look after the children, the result is that they avoid producing children. On the other hand in the joint family system there is no such problem, because even if both the husband and wife are employed, there are many elder ladies who can look after the children and as such the couple does not wish to check fertility.

(iv) **Social Status of the Women:** Fertility also depends on social status of the women. In societies where women are confined only to household jobs, these are considered suitable only for producing children and as such those women who can produce good children are held in high esteem. Obviously in such societies fertility is very high as compared with the societies where the women are expected to participate in all walks of life along with men. Obviously in such societies the women want to limit their children. Similarly educated and employed women also avoid having big families.

(v) **Political Factors Influencing Fertility:** In a country like India where there is population explosion, every political party in power is likely to take effective steps for checking population. Each government then provides incentives as well as disincentives to check fertility and birth rate. Facilities are then provided to those who go in for sterilization or similar other measures.

(vi) **Attitude towards Children:** In many societies it is believed that the children are the real possession of family and society. They are the source of strength and power and can stand with parents at the time of difficulty. Similarly it is with the help of male children alone that family can pull on and parental line can continue to exist. In such societies every effort is made to have male children and when there are girls only, the couple continues to go on giving birth to children till boy is born. When the attitude towards children is thus positive, family size goes on increasing and then there is no check on fertility.

(vii) **Death Rate:** Another factor which influences fertility is death rate. In the past the rate of child mortality was very high. It used to be almost sure and certain that at least one or two children will die. Accordingly the fertility was high so that a cushion was provided for the children who would die at some later stage. Today the society has controlled many diseases which used to kill the children, now no longer show their fatal strength. Accordingly the parents now wish to have only as many number of children, as they wish to have. This has considerably influenced fertility.

(viii) **Intellectual Freedom:** In fact there are many factors which influence fertility and it will be difficult to enumerate each. These can be political, economic, social and religious factors. Income, education, caste, occupation, nationality and community to which a person belongs can be some other causes which effect fertility. According to **Prof. Thompson and Lewis** growth of intellectual freedom in other fields of life during 19th and 20th centuries has also considerably influenced fertility. According to them, "We believe however that this gradual emancipation of the human mind from the fetters, tradition and dogma was a very important factor in changing the attitudes of many towards people to reproduction in the 18th and 19th centuries. To ignore the change in the general intellectual atmosphere which made women demand rights as persons is to overlook one of the underlying causal factors in the decline in the birth rate".

(ix) **Role of Science:** In influencing fertility science has played its own role. Prof. Thompson and Lewis make us believe that without proper appreciation of value of science, use of contraception would not have developed so quickly as it has developed today. In their own words, "Had there not been a rapidly growing appreciation of the value of science in making good health possible and of the importance of economic minimum for maintaining a healthy family, the voluntary control of the size of the family by the use of contraception almost certainly could not have developed as rapidly as it did from about 1850 to the present time."

(x) **Desire to Maintain Status:** In every society there is keen desire that social status once attained should not only be maintained but also be improved. Not only this, but there is also a desire that the children should have still better and improved status, so that the family can go ahead in the eyes of the world. In the words of Prof. Thompson and Lewis,

"Therefore, in a society where there is strong competition to maintain and/or improve social status and where safe and simple means of preventing conception are widely known, the restriction of the size of family is likely to spread rather rapidly."

**Prof. Donald J. Bogue's views about Fertility:** Prof. Donald J. Bogue has also discussed some of the important factors which influence and effect fertility. Among others he has made mention of marital status i.e. the age at which marriage takes place, after the marriage whether the couple lives a happy or unhappy life, whether the couple wishes to enjoy life or their relations are strained or they live a separated or divorced life and so on.

- Then another factor about which attention has been drawn is what the level of educational attainment of the society is on the one hand and that of the particular family on the other.
- Fertility also depends on the rural living and urbanization. In a country like India where vast majority lives in the rural areas, the fertility is bound to be different as compared with the fertility of the population living in the urban areas. In the former case the fertility is sure to be higher, as compared with the latter.
- Prof. Bogue is also of the view that region in which the people live, also influences fertility. The people of hot region are more fertile as compared with the people of cold region. He has proved this by saying that cold regions of the world are less populated, as compared with hot ones.
- Then he believes that fertility is influenced by the occupation of the head of the family. The people with good occupations are likely to check fertility, whereas those with menial occupations are likely to have more children. He has related this to income also. According to him where income is low, fertility goes up, but income is not very high, then the fertility is the lowest, but when income considerably increases with that fertility goes up. He is of the opinion that it is wrong to think that when the family is rich the number of children will be less.
- Prof. Bogue has also linked fertility with the occupation of the women. On the whole employed women are likely to produce   fewer children as compared with the unemployed

women. Even those who are employed among them social scientists, accountants and auditors, designer, professors etc. are likely to have less fertility as compared with the women engaged in other professions.

- Another factor which according to him effects fertility is extent of the use of contraceptives. These days their use has become quite common. Their use checks fertility and helps in adjusting the period between the births of two children.

## Related studies on the theme

Undoubtedly in the context of social research, the review of literature and pre-assessment of studies is an important ladder because without doing review we cannot provide smooth management. Review of literature tells investigator on what subject, sub topics the studies have been carried out, what type of research design, methods, tools and techniques were used in them along with difficulties faced and resolved by them. It is true that each social problem has relation with country, time and situations. From this view point assessment of old studies is not only important but essential too. In the changed environment in present study how many problems may occur, which methods tools and techniques would be useful to study, which aspects, stages and factors had been studied before and which aspects are left over and now which perceptive is outstanding to the present study. How to do study so that research work might be simple and easy in objective form and save money, time and labour? This all is known to researches by doing review of literature. **Singh, S.P.[23] (1975:14)** highlighted on the fruitfulness of review of literature. According to him, after relation of the topic it is not necessary but essential for the research problem in connection with review of literature pertaining to research topic because it helps :-

1. It develops in sight and knowledge in reference of research problem in the mind of research.
2. He learns adequate knowledge in relation to used research techniques and methods.
3. Review of literature helps in formulating hypothesis and evolving structure schedule.

4.     He does not commit error to repeat the research problem, which has already been carried out.

The comment in this direction of **Basin, F.H.**[24] **(1962:42)** is illustrative. He says in every research study related literature and per assessment studies is important stair of research scheme because every research work to be cleared and difficulties resolved by review of literature both the problems of research complexity and unclearness are resolved. It is because of the review of literature that how to collect valid and reliable information. The following are the usefulness of review of literature.

1.     Research develops general knowledge about research problem.

2.     Research synopsis and useful methods and techniques are cleared in the mind of researcher that how to edit research work.

3.     By review of literature investigator correct his miss concepts, doubts and illusions regarding research study and side-by-side work becomes simple to conduct activities. Thus he gets new orientation to develop his insight. **Prof. Borg, J.P.**[25] **(1963:48)** also highlighted on importance of review of literature. He says, review of literature enables researcher in such an extent so that he may be able to seek knowledge about already carried out the work which had done and could study them? To do so, investigator gets clear orientation for research on the basis of acquired knowledge and able to select adequate instruments and methods. On the other hand **Prof. Staufer S.**[26] **(1962:73)** tells that in the absence of excessive study and assessment of old literature, any sort of study is just like a firing in darkness. Without review of literature, research work cannot go ahead. Till researcher does not acquire knowledge about the area in which studies have been completed he cannot select the topic of the research not prepare the synopsis of research study nor provide speed to his investigation. The main reason of the objectives of the study is to bring innovation after thinking. The contribution of **Pursotum**[27] **(1991:110)** cannot be is dated regarding review of literature according to him, generally there are three domains of knowledge (1) To collect knowledge (2) Transmit knowledge and (3)

Increase knowledge. These three fundamental elements are especially important in research studies.

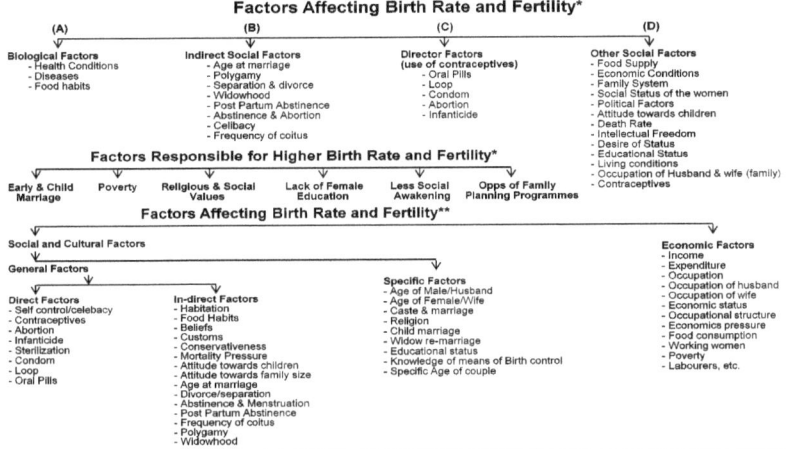

**Factors Affecting Birth Rate and Fertility***

| (A) | (B) | (C) | (D) |
|---|---|---|---|
| Biological Factors | Indirect Social Factors | Director Factors (use of contraceptives) | Other Social Factors |
| - Health Conditions | - Age at marriage | - Oral Pills | - Food Supply |
| - Diseases | - Polygamy | - Loop | - Economic Conditions |
| - Food habits | - Separation & divorce | - Condom | - Family System |
| | - Widowhood | - Abortion | - Social Status of the women |
| | - Post Partum Abstinence | - Infanticide | - Political Factors |
| | - Abstinence & Abortion | | - Attitude towards children |
| | - Celibacy | | - Death Rate |
| | - Frequency of coitus | | - Intellectual Freedom |
| | | | - Desire of Status |
| | | | - Educational Status |
| | | | - Living conditions |
| | | | - Occupation of Husband & wife (family) |
| | | | - Contraceptives |

**Factors Responsible for Higher Birth Rate and Fertility***

| Early & Child Marriage | Poverty | Religious & Social Values | Lack of Female Education | Less Social Awakening | Opps of Family Planning Programmes |
|---|---|---|---|---|---|

**Factors Affecting Birth Rate and Fertility****

Social and Cultural Factors

General Factors

Economic Factors
- Income
- Expenditure
- Occupation

| Direct Factors | In-direct Factors | Specific Factors | - Occupation of husband |
|---|---|---|---|
| - Self control/celebacy | - Habitation | - Age of Male/Husband | - Occupation of wife |
| - Contraceptives | - Food Habits | - Age of Female/Wife | - Economic status |
| - Abortion | - Beliefs | - Caste & marriage | - Occupational structure |
| - Infanticide | - Customs | - Religion | - Economics pressure |
| - Sterilization | - Conservativeness | - Child marriage | - Food consumption |
| - Condom | - Mortality Pressure | - Widow re-marriage | - Working women |
| - Loop | - Attitude towards children | - Educational status | - Poverty |
| - Oral Pills | - Attitude towards family size | - Knowledge of means of Birth control | - Labourers, etc. |
| | - Age at marriage | - Specific Age of couple | |
| | - Divorce/separation | | |
| | - Abstinence & Menstruation | | |
| | - Post Partum Abstinence | | |
| | - Frequency of coitus | | |
| | - Polygamy | | |
| | - Widowhood | | |

* Hans Raj ; Fundamentals of Demography : Population Studies with special reference to India (Fertility) Surjeet Pub. Delhi, 1978, p. 59-68.
** Chahar K.S. ; Socio-economic Factors of urban Fertility : A case study of Mathura city of U.P., 1996, p. 65.

These attempts keep researchers very nearer to reality. The contribution in the store of knowledge and strength in awareness makes possible the human made endeavours. In the same way in the process of research, "Review of Literature" is such an important scientific ladder of research entrepreneur which is stylized in the uterus of present. In order words individuals compose new knowledge through research on the bases of his old awareness and black white knowledge. So, the researcher has also made 'Review of Literature' given as under:

Modernization involves changes not only in the material culture of society but also in its belief system, values, and the way of life on the whole. It is a process of the transformation of a society from its backward outlook to a forward-looking, progressive and prosperous structural build-up, but modernity is the state of change in the attitudes, while modernization is the process of change.

'Modernity has been defined by a variety of indices, such as level of education, exposure to mass media, urban residence, type of occupation, ownership of modern household items or degree of adherence to religious or cultural traditions. When individuals or populations are classified on a scale of modernity, an inverse relationship between modernity and fertility is found (Fawcett, 1970).[28]

From the Harvard Project, Smith and Inkeles (1966) assumed that "modernity would emerge as a complex but coherent set of psychic dispositions manifested in general qualities such as a sense of efficacy, readiness for new experience, and interest in planning, linked in turn, to certain dispositions to act in institutional relations as in being; in active citizen, valuing science, maintaining one's autonomy in kinship matters and accepting birth control".

Williamson[29] (1969) from the Harvard Project data concluded that subjective efficacy and ideal family size function more as independent determinants than as intervening variables. It is one of the most important studies yet undertaken to clarify the linkages, via, both social and psychological routes and between modernity and fertility. KahI (1968) conducted another cross-national study on modernism, which is similar to the Harvard Project in its conceptual and methodological approach. He developed a scale of values that differentiate between modern and traditional men in Brazil and Mexico. A consistent inverse relationship between degree of modernism and size of ideal family was shown formost occupational groups, but only a few of the differences were statistically significant. The cross-cultural work of McClelland on the achievement motive is another attempt to understand an aspect of modernity among women (McClelland, 1961; McClelland and Winter, 1969).

Modernity has also been found to be related to birth limitation. The study of Korean family planning behaviour by Chung, Palmore and Lee (1972) showed a positive relationship of modern attitudes to contraceptive practice. A study by Coombs and Freedman (1979) examined some of the connecting links between modernization in a developing society, particularly urbanization, increased education for women and preferences for a desired number of children. Following Smith and Inkeles, Fawcett and Bomstein (1973) presented three themes of modernization reflected in personality orientation which are considered particularly relevant to family planning and fertility change, subjective efficacy, orientation towards time and openness to change. Many studies supported a negative relationship between fertility and an advanced level of modernization as a social variable (Fawcett and Bomstein, 1973; Ryder, 1959; United Nations, 1953; Adelman and Morris, 1966). Kahl (1968) reported that the family system in Rio de

Janeiro appears to be more modern than the family system in Mexico City and this, he claims, accounts for the wider difference between provincial and metropolitan fertility norms in Brazil compared to Mexico.

Both the Indianapolis study (Kiser and Whelpton, 1953; Kiser, 1962) and Princeton study (Westoff et al. 1961; Westoff, et al., 1963) have attempted to show how differences in family structure produce differential fertility.

**Value Orientations:**

Beginning with the Indianapolis Study of social and psychological factors affecting fertility (Whelpton and Kiser, 1946, 1950, 1952, 1954, and 1958) almost every investigation showed socio-economic status as the predominant determinant variations in fertility. **Clifford[30] (1971)** stated that 'the complex of socio-economic forces exert their influence on fertility through the determination and reinforcement of certain value orientations. According to Kluckhohn (1950) a "value orientation" is "a generalized and organized conception influencing behaviour, nature, man's place in it, man's relation to man, and the desirable and non-desirable as they may relate to man-environment and inter-human relations". Two polar types of values namely, 'traditional' and 'modern' were distinguished by Kahl (1968). According to Kahl, traditional values are compulsory in their force, sacred in their tone. They call for fatalistic acceptance of the world as it is Modern values is rational and secular, permit choice, clarify efficiency and stress individual responsibility". Those who value mastery over nature, the future, doing, individual responsibility tend to be characterized by low fertility' (Spengler, 1966).

Planning Orientation:

Planning orientation is an important element of modernization figures in Kahl's, Inkeles and Smith's concept of conceptualization and operationalization of modern man or modernism. According to Kahl the modern man is an activist, he believes in making plans in advance for the important events and phases of his life and has a sense of security that can usually bring these plans to fruition. Inkeles (1966) insists, "The more modern man is oriented towards planning and organizing and believes in it as a way of handling life". It was noticed that those who observe planning in different aspects of family life also show a tendency to plan their family size (U.N. Asian Population Studies Series-No. 16, 1974). In a stuck, Reddy (1986) found that those who normally plan for the quality of life are more likely to have low fertility.

**Faith in Man's Efforts:**

Faith in man's capacity to influence events, including faith in predictability of social order forms a part of the modernism theme. The belief that man can exert control over his environment has been recognized as a significant variable for differentiating traditional societies from modernized societies (Kluckhohn, 1950; Kluckhohn and Strodbeck, 1961). In one way or another, all important studies of modernism have obtained measures of people's beliefs about their personal capacity to control what appear them as observe of how much they feel controlled by luck and supernatural beings. (Lerner[32],1958, Inkeles, 1966, Back, 1967, Kahl, 1968; Rogers, 1969).

Value of Children:

In literal sense, 'value' refers to the degree of worth or excellence assigned to or derived from an object. **Wolman[33] (1973)** revealed that values are considered as attitudes, motivations, objects, measurable quantities, substantive areas of behaviour, affective laden customs or traditions and relationships such as those between individuals, groups, objects and events. In the 'Value of Children' study (Arnold et al. 1975), the value referred to a hypothetical net worth of children with positive value (satisfactions) balanced against negative values (costs). In micro-economic theories of fertility developed by a number of economists (Leibenstein, 1957; Becker, 1960; Easterlin, 1969; Robinson and Hor Jacher, 1971), child-bearing decisions were equated to consumer choices, emphasing income and price variables as controlling factors. A few studies were conducted on economic costs and benefits of children (Mueller, 1972; O'Donell, 1974; Cramer, 1975, Usha Rani, 1983).

**Educational Aspirations for Children:**

The preference for smaller families in the developed countries is said to be the consequence of the reduction in the value of children and increase in the costs of children to their parents **(Moni Nag. 1980)[34]**. The direct economic costs of children in terms of education, housing, food and many other items increased with urbanization (Banks, 1954; Blake 1972). According to Simon (1960), among all the items of costs of children, the greatest increase associated with industrialization was the educational costs. He further pointed out that although the benefit of education was perceived quickly by middle class industrialists. The working class was also not too late in recognizing the need for education in its political fight against exploitation.

**Status of Women:**

Blake (1974) speaks of the 'special interest' which women's status has for demographers explaining that "the nature of women's position and the variations in its articulation with the status of men, influence important variables with which students of population are concerned, in particular reproductive behaviour and the size and the quality of labour force". The status of women is defined as a conjunction of position she occupies as a worker, student, wife, mother etc. at any point of time. The prestige attached to these positions plus the rights and duties expected accordingly **(Sipilia, 1975)**[35]. Her status in society can be determined by her composite stains which can be ascertained from the extent of control that she has over her own life derived from access to knowledge, economic resources arid the degree of autonomy enjoyed in the process of decision-making and choice at crucial points in her life cycle (United Nations, 1975). It has been found that the fertility performance of a woman is greatly determined by the social status that she enjoys in the society by virtue of her education, economic position, freedom for the selection of marriage partners and decision-making. It is further mentioned that a negative association exists between the fertility of women and her social status. The World Population Plan of Action (United Nations, 1974), recognizes that reduction in national population growth rates will depend on broad based socio economic changes including modifications in the status and roles of women. Ridley (1968) stated that labour force participation of women leads to a more egalitarian relationship between husbands and wives, which in turn, is said to be related to lower fertility. Similarly, Weller (1969) stated that wives manifest lower fertility in wife dominant and egalitarian families rather than in husband dominant families. Jordan (1976) concluded that "with respect to formal education, it may not be education person which influences a woman to have a smaller family, but the association of education with certain other social and environmental factors which ultimately decreases fertility. These factors may be late marriage, exposure to new ideas, increased employment opportunities, greater interest in events outside the home and the like.

**Decision-making and Fertility:**

Lewin (1951) visualized the act of deciding as a transition from a state of indecisiveness to a state of definiteness, where ones choice gains dominance, forces favouring one choice dominate while forces favoring other choices become zero or diminish. Since communication between partners is crucial for the achievement of effective birth planning, the values, attitudes and degree of information which men, possess determine to a considerable extent the outcome of the decision making process of the couple especially in patriarchal societies where the husband is the primary agent of family responsibility **(Hollerbach, 1980)**[36]. As outlined by Hollerbach (1982) the key elements involved in fertility decisions are the demand for children, the supply of children and the costs of fertility regulation.

The aggregations of decision-making in various areas of family life require that they be associated with some general authority pattern in the family. Decision making patterns may reflect the specific interests, involvement and time constraints of each spouse rather than an explicit family power structure (Douglas and Wind, 1978). According to Coombs and Fernandez (1978), communication and decision making on issues relating to sexuality and fertility are not synonymous with decision making on instrumental or impersonal issues, such as expenditures and leisure time activities. The responsibilities of both husband and wife on family decision-making may reflect the influence of sex role expectations, since modesty or vanity biases have been reported frequently (Douglas and Wind, 1978). The approach by Olson and Cromwell (1975), to study the power examines the relationship between prior discussion of family size or family planning and the attainment of fertility goal through the use of contraception. A model developed by the same authors and that of Shedlin and Ljolierbeach (1978) is well applied to the outcome of fertility decision-making particularly in the decision to use contraception or to go for abortion. Further, the outcomes of decision-making are distinguished as passive decisions and active decisions, the latter being further subdivided into unilateral/ open, unilateral and joint decisions.

48

## Perception of Infant Mortality and Fertility:

High infant and child mortality is considered as one of the deterrent factors in the adoption of small family norms in developing countries because successful reproduction requires high fertility to offset high mortality (Davis, 1945; Notesteine, 1945). Since the probability of infant survival is low in developing countries, parents may require producing more children than necessary (desired) in the hope that at least a few would survive to adulthood. U.N. Department of Economic and Social Affairs (1973) notes, 'evidence accumulates that reduction of infant mortality may be a necessary prerequisite to the acceptance of family planning. Couples will not wish to prevent pregnancies until they have some assurance that the children they already have will survive". In high mortality societies, parents may fear the loss of children, given their personal experience with death in the family and community. They may, therefore, produce more children than they would otherwise have in order to insure themselves against possible risks of child loss. One's perception of community mortality is rather vague and ambiguous **(Chaudhury, 1982)**[37]. **Heer and Smith (1968)**[38] assumed that parents accurately assess prevailing mortality and procreate until they are 95 per cent certain of at least having one son alive by the time the father is 66. Very few studies actually measured parents' perception of infant mortality audits effect on fertility and even when these were measured, the responses were unreliable (Stycos 1965a; Taylor and Takuya, 1971). Heer and Wu (1975) using data from Taiwan developed an index of perception of child survival and found it negatively associated with subsequent birth. Respondents with a low perception of child survival go on to have about 0-24 more additional children after adjustment for other variables than those with higher perception. Some attitudinal surveys, however, pointed out those respondents who believe that current child mortality is lower than in the past are also those who desire a smaller number of children (Cassen, 1976). Taylor (1976) mentioned that those who perceive of increased chances of child survival use contraception more than twice that of women who do not share such a view. However, Heer and Wu (1975) and Rutstein (1971) did not find any association between perception of child survival and use of contraception.

Karsten Hank in his article (2007) on Parental Gender Preferences and Reproductive behaviour: A review of the recent literature reviews various theoretical approaches towards an explanation of parental gender preferences and empirical findings from developing as well as from industrialized countries, focusing on the role of gender preferences in reproductive decisions. Although various attempts have been made to shed light on the mechanisms underlying the observed patterns of sex preferences for children, a frilly satisfying theoretical explanation is still not at hand. Empirically, a distinct and table preference for at least one child of each sex can be observed as a common pattern of parental sex preferences across many different social, economic and cultural contexts. Further and ideally multidisciplinary research that helps to improve our understanding of this phenomenon is highly desirable.

Lopamudra Paul and P.M. Kulkami (2006) have presented a paper on 'The Dynamics of fertility transition in west Bengal in India in European population conference 2006 held in Liverpool, United Kingdom. According to them the term fertility transition appeared in the literature in the early 1970s and was given a precise meaning as change from natural fertility to family limitation. Presently, India is passing through fertility transition but the timing and pace of transition has varied spatially over the country. Transition in the eastern state of West Bengal in India began well before independence, though the pace was slow for quite some time, the state is fast approaching replacement level low fertility. This paper examines the timing and nature of the transition of fertility in the state. Trends in fertility assessed using data from the Indian censuses, the Sample Registration System, and large population surveys shows a moderate fall through the 1980s and a steep drop during the 1990s. An examination of proximate determinants reveals the dominant role of contraceptive prevalence in the decline. A detailed analysis in trends in the family building process is possible from individual fertility histories. It is seen that the age of marriage has risen marginally though that is not reflected in a corresponding rise in age at first birth. Analysis of the parity progression ratios shows that the progression to the first two parities has not changed much; however, notable fall has occurred in the progression to higher parities. The transition was quite slow initially, but quickened in the 1990s. Contraceptive practice has increased substantially over the period and the tendency of limiting family after two or three children has become widespread. Contraceptive use in West Bengal has not been dominated by sterilization unlike that in most other states of India and there has been considerable resort to traditional contraception suggesting that couples have a wide choice. It appears that the family planning programme in the state was not coercive in nature and the acceptance has been mostly voluntary.

Debarati Sarkar[39] (2006) focuses on issues relating to fertility and related economic development. The observed differentials in fertility between different states are determined by different socio economic developmental indicators. In this analysis she tried to find out the relationship between fertility and development using district level data from census of 1991 and 2001 through panel data regression. Also to see, any specific effect that influences fertility. The findings show that literacy of both male and female are directly related to low fertility. Poverty is proportionately related to high fertility.

In the light of the above made observations, the researcher has got so many advantages other than clear insight regarding his study.

# REFERENCES

1.  'Fatwa' ; Sheikh Abdullah Al-qualquili; Muslim Attitudes towards Family Planning, The Population Council, New York, 1967, p.3.
2.  United Nations; The Determinants and Consequences of Population Trends, New York, p. 35.
3.  Thomas R. Malthus, Essay, Royal Economic Society, 1798, p. 11.
4.  Thomas R. Malthus; A Summary: View of the Principle of Population, Royal Economic Society, 1978, p. 114.
5.  Ralph Thomlinson; Population Dynamics, Random House Pub. Com., New York, 1965, p. 56.
6.  Kingsley Davis, "Malthus and the Theory of Population" Paul F. Lazarsfeld and Morris Hosenberg (Eds.), The Language of Social Research, New York: The Free Press, 1955, p. 541.
7.  United Nations, The Determinants and Consequences of Population Trends, Vol. I, Population Studies No. 50, 1973, p.78.
8.  United Nations, Multilingual Demographic Dictionary, New York, p.39.
9.  United Nations, Multilingual Demographic Dictionary, New York, p.38.
10. United Nations; Quoted from, Demography and Population Studies, Raj Hans Pub. Meerut, by Sharma R.N. & Sharma R.K., 1989, p.144.
11. -Kingsley Davis and Judith Blake, "Social Structure and Fertility: An Analytic Framework" Economic Development and Social Change, Vol.4, No. 3, April, 1965, pp. 211-235.
    -Kingsley Davis; The World Demographic Transition, Journal of Pol. & Social Science, Vol. 237, 1997, p. 1-11.
12. Srivastav B.K. (2007); A Survey of Fertility in a Town of Pune, Gokhale Institute Publication Pune, 2007, No. 38, (43).
13. Chahar K.S.; A study of Social Determinants of Fertility: A case study of Mathura Distt. Of U.P., Research Pub., Jaipur, 1990.

14. Sharma R.N. et.al. ; Social Demography and Population Problems; Rajhans Agencies, Ram Nagar, Meerut, 2001, p. 185.

15. John J.H.; Principles of Public Health Administration, Mosby Pub. Co. St. Louis, 1960, p. 363.

16. Kingsley Davis; "Population Policy: Will Current Programmes Succeed?" in Ashish Bose, Studies in Demography, p. 389.

17. Secretary General U-thant of the U.N.; "Declaration on Population", Studies in family planning, No. 16, Jan. 1967, p. 1.

18. Everett. M. Rogers; Communication Strategies for family planning, The Free Press, 1973, p. 152.

19. Hans Raj; Fundamentals of Demography: Population Studies with special reference to India, Surjeet Publications and Distributors, Delhi, 1978, p.319.

20. Singh S.P.; Review of Literature in Social Sciences, Alok Publ. (Pvt. Ltd.) Rajasthan, Jaipur, 1975, p. 14.

21. Basin H.F.; Literature Assessment in Applied Science, Mc-Millan Co., Madras, 1962, p. 40.

22. Borg G.P.; Observation of Literature in Social Science Research, Jain Brothers, Bombay, Andheri, 1963, p. 48.

23. Stauffer Semmuel ; Review : A Major Step in Investigations in Social Sciences; American Sociological Review, No. 23, 1962.

24. -Purushottam Roy; The Elements of Social Research, Saraswati Prakashan, Darbhanga, Bihar, 1991, p. 110.
    -Purushottam Roy & Pareek U. ; Population Growth & Family Planning measures/contraceptives, Sage Publications, Delhi, 2001, p. 63.

25. Fawcett, J.T.; Psychology and Population: Behavioural Research Issues in Fertility and Family Planning, The Population Council, New York, 1970, p. 69.

26. Willianson; Subjective efficacy as an aspect of modernization in six developing nations, unpublished Ph.D. Thesis, Harvard University, 1969.

27. Clifford, William B.; "Modern and traditional value orientations and fertility behaviour", Demography, 1971, p. 37-48.

28. Kahl, J.N.; The Measurement of Modernism: A Study of Values in Brazil and Mexico. Austin: The University of Texas Press, 1968, pp. 4, 18-20.

29. Lerner, Daniel; The Passing of Traditional Society: Modernizing the Middle East, New York, Free Press, 1958.

30. Wolman, B.B. (ed.); Dictionary of Behavioural Science, New York; Van Nostrand Reinhold Company, 1973, pp. 399-400.

31. Nag, M.; How modernization can also increase fertility, Current Anthropology, 1980, 21:27-36.

32. Sipilia, H.; "Status of Women and Family Planning", Department of Economic and Social Affairs, New York, 1975, p. 4.

33. Hollerbach, P.E.; Power in families, communication and fertility decision making, The Free Press, Glencoe, 1980.

34. Chaudhury, Rafiqul H. ; Social Aspect of Fertility: With Special Reference to Developing Countries, Vikas Publishing House, New Delhi, 1982.

35. Heer, D. and Smith, D.O.; 'Mortality level, Desired Family size and Population increase', Demography, 1968, Vol. 5, No. 1.

36. Sarkar Debarati, A Study on Fertility in a poor community, Published Research Paper "Samajik Sahyog", Quarterly Journal, Ujjain (M.P.), 2006, p. 47-53.

❖❖❖❖❖

# CHAPTER 2
# Research Design & Methodology

"Science goes with the method, not with the subject matter."[1]
* *Stuart Chase; The Proper Study of Mankind, 1956, p. 6.*

"There is no short-cut to truth, no way to gain knowledge of the universe except through the gateway of scientific method."[2]
* *Karl Person; The Grammar of Science, A&C, Black Pub. Co., London, 1911, p.1.*

"The development of each subject depends upon the appropriate development of its methodology."[3]
* *Festinger L. & Daniel; Research Methods in Behavioural Science, The Free Press, Glencoe, 1976, p. 30.*

As the human being is the highest composition of God, in the same way human society and various social phenomena are the highest contribution of man. The human being is intellectual, full of curiosity and has thrust for knowledge, therefore, it is truly said that human being not only studies the nature but also studies himself.

The study of earth, plants, wind, rivers and sea presents wonderful experiences, educate human being and fulfill his curiosities of the art and science, but the study of himself, his behaviour or social events are very interesting, excessively wonderful and full of uniqueness in nature.

This sort of study is not subjective by nature, but the truth can be attained only by observations, experiments and empirical based activities. In relation to social events the observation of truth is social research. Research in all fields of human activities means continued search for knowledge and understanding. But, not all knowledge and understanding is scientific.

"Scientific research is essentially made up to two elements- (1) Observation by which knowledge of certain facts is obtained through sense perception and (2) Reasoning by which the meaning of these facts, their inter-relation and their relation to the existing body of scientific knowledge are ascertained as far as the existing sate of knowledge and investigator's ability permit".[4]

If both of these elements are available in investigation of social facts, then it is called social research. In this outlook social research is empirical method to solve any social problem, to verify the hypotheses, to seek cause of new problem and to co-relate the cause and effect relationship with various new problems.

This empirical method ought to be such which fulfills the terms and conditions of science and with the help of it, subject of research may be verified. In brief, for the sake of new knowledge systematic endeavors are called social research.

Now it is clear that social research according to regulation of science indicates about the human activities, which strengthen our knowledge pertaining to cause and effect about the phenomenon. The more exploratory thing about social research is the method, which is based on observation, classification and analysis of information's. In this context, **Mrs. Young**[5]

**(1960:44)** said that, "We may define social research as a scientific undertaking which by means of logical and systematized methods, aims to discover new facts or old facts to analysis their sequences, inter-relationship, causal explanations and the natural laws which govern them". Therefore **Moser**[6] **(1961)**, said that "Systematized investigation to gain new knowledge about social phenomenon and problems, we can call social research".

Social research is not a simple work that is why individual cannot perform it. Merely bookish knowledge is not sufficient for it. Some other internal and external characteristics are essential because social research is concerned with the social problems and social problems are abstract, changeable, complex and individual oriented, thus, their study is more difficult than that of natural sciences. It is unique to study the social problem, the study of human by human as the subject of this research study is **"Effect of Modernity on Fertility among Muslim Women of Shikohabad City".**

**Kerlinger, F.N.**[7] **(1964:4)** revealed, "The developments of the subject of study is dependent on its development of research methods, not on context".

Therefore, the discussion of research method **Jahoda**[8] **(1950)** divided them in Normative and applied methods of research. In general **normative** objectives produce theoretical knowledge and **applied** objectives provide utilitarian knowledge.

**Karl Pearson**[9] **(1911)** further explains this situation in his words, "In Normative research, original principal and rules are explored in references to social lives, problems and phenomenon, which indicates what should be done by investigator, on the contrary, in applied research, treatment of problem is submitted through deep study of problem in relation to human behaviour and applicable suggestions are given". Therefore **Kerlinger** divided research work in to the three categories:
(1) Original/Fundamental/Pure Research (2) Action Research (3) Applied/ Behavioural Research.

Research Design*:

Research Design, as any other concept and process, has been defined and applied by different Social Scientists in different terms and ways. But there has been one thing common in all these definitions and explanations that is their emphasis on systematic methodology in collecting accurate information's and data for studying the problem and its interpretation, synthesization and generalization of data collected and information's collected with precision of time and optimum use of financial resources in social research procedure. In simple words "Design" means 'to plan' or to take decisions about the format of research project in advance. And a research Design is the plan, structure and strategy of investigation conceived so as to tackle and encounter the research problem more efficiently and accurately. Hence, a research design is overall a plan or scheme or programme of the research including an outline of everything the investigator will do, from writing the hypotheses and their operational implications to the procedure of collecting data and then final analysis and interpretation of data. The structure of the research is more specific and includes the outline, the scheme, the model diagram and the operations of the variables and all of this depends on the nature of the problem under study.

**A good research design may be clarified in the following words:**

A research design is the state, structure and strategy of any investigation conceived so as to tackle

---

*(i) "A Research Design is the arrangement of conditions for collection and analysis of data in a manner that aims to combine relevance to the research purpose with economy in procedure".
* *Joheda C.S. (et.al.);Research Method in Social Relations, Rinehart & Winston Holt, London, 1963, p. 50.*
(ii)"A Research Design is the logical and Systematic Planning & directing of a piee of research".
    * *Young P.V. ; Scientific Social Survey & Research, Printce Hall of India Pvt. Ltd., New Delhi, 1975, p. 131*

and encounter the research problem more efficiently and accurately. It seeks to obtain answers to research questions of objectives, problem of hypothesis is more efficiently and to control variance (So that research question can be answer more accurately). The plan is the overall scheme or programme of the research including an outline of everything, the investigator will do from writing the hypothesis and their operational implications to the procedure of collecting data and the final analysis and interpretation of data. The structure of the research is more specific and includes the outline, the scheme, the paradigms (Model) of the operation of the variables. The strategy is also more specific and includes the method of design to be used; to collect the primary data and the tools to analysis and interpret the data. The strategy implies how the research objectives will be reached and how the problems encountered in the research will be tackled. Therefore, here the researcher would like to mention the classification of research methodology. There are two types of research methodology in social sciences: Empirical and Normative. Empirical deals with realistic attempts to analyze and interprets the real behaviour of social animals and normative method directs what should be done by a researcher? In this method some standards are established to evaluate the research work. Research works are classified into three categories by The Scholars: (i) Fundamental or pure research (ii) Applied or behavioural Research and (iii) Action Research.

This work of the researcher is related to applied and action types of research. The attempt is made to understand the socio-economic conditions of the respondents selected for the study purpose and conditions of the universe under study also. **Kapil**[10] (et.al.), have stated four major steps to conduct a social research:

(i) Working Hypothesis (ii) Observation and recording of data and (iii) Generalization. But **Arnold Brachet**[11] **(1970:12)** has suggested eleven steps for research procedure: Observation, description, measurement, inductive/deductive generalization, explanation, logical, verification of data, co-relation and hypothesis rejection. But as a matter of fact, a research work is conducted on three major steps: (i) The Problem (ii) Hypothesis (iii) Research Design. Research work started from the determination of the problem and it ends generalization. In this way the research work depends upon the nature of the study problem, objectives of the study and testing of the hypotheses framed before starting of the work.

Now it is clear that there are many kinds of social research designs and the investigator in order to achieve his target selects one of them which is most suitable in his opinion and as the type of design is determined the nature of research work and its objectives are clear. Like if we know the research design is exploratory, than it is automatically understood that investigation of inherent reasons and causes of some social event is the main objective of the research work. The main objectives of all research are achievement of knowledge. This knowledge can be attained by various means. So research design is also of several types according to objectives. Mostly, Exploratory, Descriptive and Experimental research designs are used in sociological studies. In this research study exploratory and explanatory designs have been used.

Jahoda[12] said that, "Exploratory research design in necessary to obtain the experience which will be helpful in formulating relevant hypothesis for more definite investigation". To study the "Effect of Modernity on Fertility among Muslim Women of Shikohabad City of Firozabad district of U.P." the researcher has selected this design for his study. For example if we want to study the status and position of rural women then it would be necessary to study various issues related to the problems of rural women of different categories. Thus investigator selected exploratory design in this study to observe those factors, which are responsible for uplift of the position of rural women. For the success of the research design investigator studied related review of literature, contacted all of those about whom he had heard that they had some knowledge of problem of rural women. In this way their experiences become direction for researcher. They all created internal motivation and insight and helped in the research work. There are various problems, out of which some are simple, some socio-psychological and some are related with individual, which encouraged the scholar to study them.

According to the above assumptions of the research procedure, it is necessary to determine the problem to conduct the present research, The present problem is such type of problem which is typical and based on the impact of modernity and family planning programmes on the fertility among Muslim women of Shikohabad City; Firozabad District of U.P. In fact enough and appropriate subject matter is not available on the present problem, because such type of the study has not been yet conducted from sociological view point. Therefore, the researcher has made up in the mind to frame a fine research design, having the following major steps in the formulation of Research Design[13]:-

(i)     **Selection and Statement of the problem:** The just task before the researcher is to select the topic of his own interest, design, the concepts and to develop the hypothesis.

(ii)    **Selection of the field coverage:** To decide for the universe of study and the sampling unit.

(iii)   **Organization of Personnel:** To decide the size of the research to be conducted according to the needs of the study, time and availability of money.

(iv)    **Budgeting:** To prepare a tentative outline of the major heads of expenditure.

(v)     **Data Collection:** To make a statement about the methods, tools and techniques to be used and phases of inquiry under study.

(vi)    **Analysis and interpretation of data.**

(vii)   **Drafting of Report:** Success of the project depends on the clarity of the thoughts of report.

Keeping in view the above points and non-availability of enough and appropriate subject matter regarding secondary data, the researcher has chosen Exploratory and Explanatory research designs for the study purpose. As we know that exploratory research design is used to find out the causes of social problem concerned and explanatory research design is used to explain the subject matter regarding the problem under study. To conduct any research through these research designs, a researcher can use available literature, informal interview, and non-participant observation to achieve the objectives of the study problem.

A researcher is needed the following precautions while conducting the study like other sciences, sociology depends on the scientific method. This process requires that the area of investigation be well defined, the concepts be operationalized and that hypotheses be formulated and tested through the collection and analyzing of data. The major steps of Scientific method are: [14]

1.      Appropriate selection of the problem for the study.

2.      Selection of proper methodology, tools and techniques etc.

3.      The formulation of Hypotheses and implementation of research procedure.

4.      Data collection (Primary and Secondary).

5.      Analysis and interpretation of facts.

6.      Objective attitude.

7.      Completion of study within a definite period as considered by the investigator.

Every researcher has to formulate **hypotheses*** to achieve goals and to justify the objectives of the study problem by empirical evidence. The objectives of the present study are as below:

The Objectives of the Study:

The major objective of the present study is to evaluate the impact of modernity on fertility behaviour among Muslim Women of Shikohabad city of Firozabad district of U.P; but the subsidiary (specific) objectives of this empirical study are as under:

(1)  To study the socio-economic conditions of the respondents.

(2)  To study the socio-cultural and determinants (factors) affecting fertility among Muslim women.

(3)  To study the co-relationship between educational status and fertility level among Muslim women.

(4)  To study the effects of family welfare scheme.

(5)  To give suggestions to control high fertility rate among Muslim women.

To justify and for the fulfillment of the above mentioned objectives of the proposed study problem, the following **'hypotheses'** have been formulated:

(1)  The fertility rate among Muslims is higher than the Hindus.

---

*
(i)  "A Hypothesis states that what we are looking for... a hypothesis looks forward. It is proposition which can be put to a test to determine its validity. It may seem contrary to or in accord with common sense, however, it leads to an empirical test".
 * Goode W.J. & Hatt P.K.; Methods in Social Research, Mc Graw Hill Book Co., Kongakusha Pvt. Ltd., 1952, p. 57.
 (ii) "Hypothesis is a proposition to be tested".
 * E.S. Bogardus, Sociology, Mac Millan & Co., New York, 1954, p. 551.
(iii)"The hypothesis is a tentative supposition".
 * Petter H.Mann, Methods of Sociological enquiry, Oxford, Basil Blackwell, 1968, p.38.
(iv)"Hypothesis is a provisionally tentative intelligent statement whose validity is to be tested on the basis of empirical evidence. It may prove to be correct or incorrect and significant or non-significant".
 * Singh S.D; Elements of Survey & Scientific Social Research, Raj Kamal Prakashan, Indore, 1986, p. 152.

(2)   The fertility rate among Muslim women who have gone through the process of modernization is lower than the one who are traditional.

(3)   Fertility behaviour is a function of literary, poverty and health indicators.

(4)   The aspiration for collegiate education to children would be greater in more modern respondents and their fertility would be lower than the less modern who would aspire relatively low education to their children.

(5)   The more modern respondents who would be better in observing planning (high score) tend to have fewer live births than the less modem respondents likely to observe poor planning (low score).

(6)   The more modern respondents who are more likely to make decisions in the family jointly with wives (high score) would tend to have lower fertility than the less modern respondents who are more likely to make decisions by themselves ignoring their spouses (low score).

(7)   The more modern respondents who are more likely to accord high status to women (high score) would tend to have lower fertility than the less modern respondents likely to give low status to women (low score).

(8)   A greater proportion of the more modern than the less modern respondents would perceive the current incidence of infant mortality as low when compared with the situation prevailed 5 years ago, and the former would tend to have lower fertility than the latter.

(9)   A greater proportion of the more modern respondents would effectively plan the timing of birth of their children compared to the less modern respondents.

(10)  The percentage of adopters of contraceptives would be higher in the more modern group as compared to the less modern group.

The above mentioned/formulated hypotheses will be tested by the empirical evidence and by the calculations of the following 'Statistical Tests':

(i)     **Chi-Square ($X^2$) test:**

$E = \dfrac{ER \times C}{G.T.}$ from this formula; the values of $E_1$, $E_2$, $E_3$ and $E_4$ will be calculated.

Chi-Square ($X^2$) =

$$-\frac{(01-E_1)^2}{E_1} - \frac{(02-E_2)^2}{E_2} - \frac{(03-E_3)^2}{E_3} - \frac{(04-E_4)^2}{E_4}$$

Degree of freedom (d.f.) = (m–1) (n–1) where m and n are rows and columns respectively.

If the probable value of Chi-square ($X^2$) is less than the table value, then the formulated hypothesis will be accepted true and significant.

(ii)    **Coefficient of Variance (Q)** $= \dfrac{AD - BC}{AD + BC}$ :

If the calculated value of the coefficient of variance (Q) is between (+) 1 and (–) 1, then the formulated hypothesis will be accepted true and significant.

(iii)   **Coefficient of co-relation (r) by Spearman's rank difference method (r) = $1 - \dfrac{6\sum d^2}{N(N^2 - 1)}$**

Where:     $\sum d^2$ = Sum of the rank difference squares

N = Total number of terms

$N^2$ = Square of the total no. of terms

It the calculated value of 'coefficient of co-relation' is positive and between (±) 1; then the null hypothesis will be accepted true and significant.

**Universe of the Study & Sampling:**

Social scientist during research process faces problems of selecting research area. In context of research area researchers have different views; some says it should be small and limited, while others say it should have wide and big, but in scientific view, it should neither be too small and limited nor too big and wide because : (1) The time limitation for research work is two year, and it has to be completed within the time (2) If the area is big and wide researcher has to waste his time, money and has to do more labour in order to collect data, that's why the research area should be neither be too small, nor too big.

Keeping in view the above points, the researcher has selected Shikohabad city of Firozabad district of U.P. as the area of the present study. According to District statistics Hand Book (2010:4) The old name of Shikohabad was Mohammad Mah and Shikohabad was named after a famous emperor Dara Shikoh of the Mughal Era, the eldest brother of Aurangzeb. It is one of the tehsil headquarters of Firozabad district with a population of 107,300 (2011 census) out of which 50107 are males and 50283 females. The total number of families is 21200 in all, in which 9696 families of Muslims are residing in Shikohabad town. It is 260 kms. from Delhi in East on Delhi Hawrah Railway track as well as on Delhi- Kanpur National Highway and 198 km. from Kanpur in West. It is located at 27.1° N – 78.6° E. It has an average elevation of 163 meters i.e. 534 feet. Shikohabad is a big town and a municipal board divided into 25 wards. The literacy rate is 81.68%, which is higher than the average literacy of India. It is perhaps due to availability of more educational institutions, as there are six Post Graduate Colleges in the town and many more high schools and Intermediate Collages within the limits of town. Shikohabad falls under Taj Trapezium Zone.

Sample Design:

The sample unit for the present study will be the household having eligible couple(s) with one or more living children and wife not less than 15 year and not exceeding 49 years of age at the time of survey.

A stratified proportionate simple random sampling design will be used in the study. The area of

66

study, Shikohabad town will be stratified on the basis of the existing municipal wards. Lists of households satisfying the above criteria will be prepared ward-wise based on eligible couples registered, which will be crosschecked and updated with the assistance of urban family planning workers.

From these lists a required number of household will be selected randomly by applying the weights to give fair representation to each ward, the weight being the ratio of number of households in a given ward to the total number of households in the universe. The number of sample households for each ward will be computed using the formula:

$$ni = \frac{Ni}{\Sigma Ni} \times n$$

Where

Ni = Number of eligible households in the given ward

$\Sigma Ni$ = Total number of eligible households in the universe

N = Sample size

**Thus the researcher has chosen 300 Muslim married couples having one or more living children below 49 years by purposive sample method as respondents for the study.**

Smith and Inkeles (1966), developed standardized instruments to measure the modernity of individuals, Kahl (1968) developed a conceptual model to differentiate modern and traditional men in Brazil and Mexico. The recent development of the "Intermediate variable" approach (Bongaarts, 1978) has introduced an intervening state into this analysis. Fertility is now seen as being directly influenced by a set of proximate determinants. Modernization in turn, operates only indirectly on fertility through these determinants (Bongaarts, 1978; 106). The present study will be based on the conceptual model shown below:

# CONCEPTUAL FRAME WORK

## DIMENSIONS OF MODERNITY AMONG WOMEN

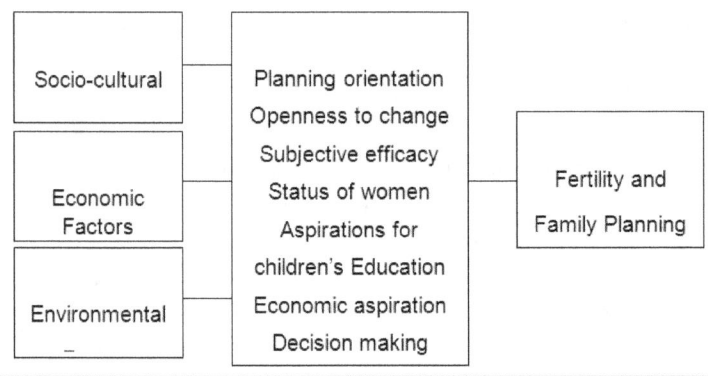

Interview Schedule:

For the collection of data an interview schedule will be developed on the basis of extensive review of available literature and discussion with experts in the field. The schedule will be divided into different sections viz., personal information, marriage, family size norm, value of children, perception of infant mortality, faith in man's efforts, openness to change, planning orientation, aspiration for education of children, decision-making in the family, status of women, motives on family limitation, contraception, achievement and economic particulars. The schedule consists of factual, structured, openness and multiple choice statements. For measuring attitudes, a Likert type scale with five responses Strongly Agree, Agree, Undecided, Disagree and Strongly Disagree will be used. The three point scale-agree, Undecided and Disagree will also be used wherever necessary. Since attitude cannot be measured accurately on the basis of responses to anyone statement, several statements are included relating to the same dimension of modernization.

**Data Collection:**

Survey will be mostly confined to the wife, but husband will also be contacted for collecting information on certain items, like pregnancy history and contraceptive practices. Thus, couple as a unit will be interviewed for the present study, which will be an improvement in the methodology of fertility study as most of the studies conducted hitherto interviewed either males or females alone.

The investigator himself will do the collection of data. Good report was established with the respondents seeking the cooperation of the multipurpose health workers, leaders of the community and members of certain voluntary organizations.

## Measurement of Variables:

In the proposed study children ever born will be the main dependent variable. Family size norms (ideal, desired and additional) and adoption of contraceptives will be the other dependent variables. Age of the respondents wives at the time of survey is, treated as the control variable since fertility as well as contraception will have positive association with present age of the mother. All other variables will be treated as independent variables.

The analysis of data will be carried out using computer facility. The collected data will be edited and coded. Means and percentages will be computed. Simple and multiple tables will be prepared. Step-wise multiple regression analysis will be done to measure the individual contribution of the independent variables in explaining the total variance in fertility.

Sources of Data:

Without primary and secondary information's and data, social Investigator is really like a handicapped person. The success of research depends on how much real dependable and appropriate information's are collected from the reliable sources. Therefore the information cannot be renovated in the field of social research. The information is not of single type, they are of many forms. The knowledge of different forms of data is essential for successful investigation. If the researcher does not know that from which source, which type of information's can be obtained then he has to wander this side and that side and his precious time and labour will be wasted. Thus the knowledge of various sources of data is necessary for a research investigation.

In social research various types of information are needed. They are classified in two forms: first primary data and secondary data. Those fundamental information's which are collected in the field by face to face relationship with the respondents of research subject through interview or schedule or direct observation are primary data. Palmer said," Such sorts of Individuals not only have ability to explain problem related to the subject but also indicate about internal important steps in social process and observable curves. **Mrs. Young (1960:127)** "classified sources of information into two Categories: documentary and field source."[15]

In this research study, researcher is keeping in mind, the problems of family welfare and fertility among rural women preferred primary source of data. Field observations were made to encounter the study. Apart from primary information, documentary sources related books, primary health centers, newspapers, doctors, nurses, Asha Bahin, A.N.M.S. as evidence are also consulted because there is lack of secondary data and if available, they are not adequate and reliable.

To observe scientifically, findings in social research about social phenomenon, scientific facts are not merely estimates but objective and scientific results based on facts and extract information's. Thus it is clear that the fundamental condition of social research is collection of real and true information's. For this, scientific devices are essential. It is because of empirical techniques (Schedule, Interview and Observation) through which data are collected, is called tools and techniques of data collection. **According to Moser (1960)[16]**, "Techniques are those accepted and systematized devices for a social scientist which are used to obtain reliable data related to his study."

Methods of data Collection:

Indeed the base of social research is reliable data, real information's and facts. In sociology the interview and observation are the techniques of the study of social phenomenon. In this study, the investigator has used 'interview-schedule' as a tool for data collection. For this, the researcher has adopted the following process for interview:

The researcher has conducted personal interview with 300 women (mothers) respondents to collect information's related to the study. Face-to face interviews with couples were conducted to collect data. Communication for the sake of research according to schedule-interview; Investigator put up the aims and objectives of research study before couple respondents and requested to provide heartiest co-operation and he assured them that their information's will be kept confidential. First of all he asked about socio-demographic profile of respondents such as: name, age at marriage, caste, religion, education, occupation, marital status, issues, polygamy, etc. After that, he asked various questions related to birth control, use of contraceptives, separation, menstruation, celibacy, frequency of coitus, Abortion, infanticide, attitude towards children, awakening, religious values, etc. The Investigator noted the responses against the questions given in Interview-schedule to avoid any kind of obstacle.

**Classification of Data:**

In social research the basis of research is really the information concerned with study. These information's when collected cannot be concluded as result, nor informed anything about the subject. The mountain of information does not serve any purpose unless it is not given in systematic form. That is why classification of information's is an essential task. When we classify the collected information on the basis of their differences and similarities; it is called classification of data. In this regard **Robert E. Chaddock**[17] **(1995:43)** has stated that, "Classification is especially important in the success of social research because of many factors affect a given situation and because of the measurement show wide variation." **Conner**[18] **(1966:18)** has also highlighted on the classification in the following words, "Classification is the process of arranging things (either actually or rationally) in groups and classes according to their resemblance and affinities and gives expression to the unity of attributes that may subsist amongst a diversity of individuals."

Keeping in mind the above consideration, the researcher has systemized synchronize and limited the helps of information on the basis of big issues, characters and terms of similarity and differences proximity and distances. In this study information's are classified quantitatively or simple or multi qualitatively along with quantitatively also, so that information's may be understood and thus classification become satisfied and pure.

Tabulation of Data:

In social research, after classification of information's, the data are placed in tables. Actually tabulation, after classification is a next step in the process of analysis. With the help of it, information's become simple and clear to understand and statistical data become demonstrational. In the process, the data is kept in columns so that they can be understood. As **Jahoda and Cook**[19] has written that, "Just as coding is thought of as the technical procedure for the categorization of data so tabulation may be considered as a part of the technical process in the statistical analysis of data". It is the reason, **Ghose**[20] **(1960:94) has explained,** "Tabulation stands for the systematic and scientific presentation of quantitative data in such a form as to elucidate the problem under consideration". That's why **Young**[21] **(1960:501) says,** "Statistical tabulation is short hand of statistics because it fills attraction, adequate size, convenience of comparison, clarity appropriate to objectives of study and scientificness".

In this research study, researcher has to make data more easily understandable. He has used simple and complex tables. He also considered all necessary rules of tabulation such as: (1) Write title of tabulation (2) Size according to area of page on which it was drawn (3) Captions (4) Write information in columns (5) Keep columns in sequences (6) Division of columns (7) Total and (8) Related Comments. With this process all collected data are systemized logically and to get clear picture in tables. This helps much in statistical analysis. Tabulation makes comparative interpretation simpler. It also saves time and space and makes scientific analysis by which work becomes simpler. Researcher has adopted the above rules in his consideration and carried out the work.

Analysis and Interpretation of Data:

"Scientific analysis assumes that behind the accumulated data there is something more important and revealing than the fact themselves, that will marshaled facts when related to the whole study, to have a significant general meaning, from which valid interpretation can be drawn."[23]

The simple meaning of above statement is that the objective of cause and effect cannot clear by collecting a mountain of information's unless these collected data are systematized and then analysis and interpretation is done. The well-known mathematician **Jules Henri Poincare wrote that,** 'Science is built with facts as a house is built with stones, but a collection of facts is no more science then a heap of stones is not a house."[24]

Therefore, it is essential for science that collected data should be orderly edited and then analysis and interpretation can be done so that true knowledge may be achieved. The fundamental need of analysis and interpretation of data if were not systematized they remain meaningless and we cannot find any result from such type of data. The research study will remain half, if data are not analysed and interpreted so far. It is the only reason that **(Smt.) Young says,** "Research is a creative aspect of scientific analysis".

Social researcher does not accept that any phenomenon is independent; he accepts collected facts, present ideas and inner social philosophy of time. Therefore any empirical result can be achieved through the careful checking of collected data, their mutual relationship are thus context relation with total events. He can only succeeded by examining old concepts, challenging situation of new concepts during the process of analysis of data. In this way whatever insight he gains by process of analysis of information, he re-examines on the basis of it and achieves a solid base for interpretation of data.

That's why, real interpretation of data is not possible without adequate analysis of data and factual interpretation; any result of findings; an investigator cannot obtain. According to **(Smt.) Young[23] P.V. (1960:310),** "The function of orderly analysis to formulate a solid organization of an edifice which helps to keep collected facts in their place so, that general finding can be achieved by them". In this way without analysis of data the explanation of cause and effect relationship pertaining to any subject or phenomenon is neither possible nor any progress of science, achievement of real knowledge because on the basis of analysis and interpretation of data, real scientific rules can be formulated. Therefore, analysis and interpretation of collected data is essential to test old thesis or to certify old theories or rules.

In this research study, researcher considering all above guidance and principles in the mind, clarified the collected data and tabulated them so that it become simple and likely to be understood easily. Thus he used analysis and interpretation of data as are adopted by sociological research reports, the same is used here.

## Generalization of Data:

After collecting the primary and secondary data in enough and sufficient quantity, the researcher has followed the 'Law of Statistical Regularity'*in generalizing the data so that a concrete and objective result may be presented. The diagrammatic representation has been given, so that the study may be simple, easy, lucid, fruitful and scientific.

## Diagrammatic Presentation of Data:

The main aim and objectives of statistical method is to provide simple forms to collected data so that everybody can easily understand them as well as appropriate findings may be observed. It is often observed that by classification and tabulation of data we get systematic orderly and brief form of scattered data the effective form to demonstrate these collected data is demonstration by pictures.

For general man only data is un-understandable and complex. Therefore, one does not pay any attention to figures. On the other hand pictures are more attractive and one cannot live without effect of it. It is only the utility and mystery of popularity of data demonstration. In this regard **Prof. Boddingtons**[24] **(1961)** has written that, "A properly constructed diagram appeals to the eyes and also to the mind because it is practically clear easily understandable even by these unacquainted with the method of presentation."

In fact tabulation makes more help in scientific interpretation of data. Yet for a general man, frequencies, which are

---

*
"The Law of statistical Regularity" formulated in the mathematical theory of probability lays down that a moderately large number of items chosen at-random from among a very large group are almost sure on the average, to have the characteristics of the large group.
- *King W.I.; The Fundamentals of Statistics, Mc-Graw Hill Book Co., New York, 1975, p. 13.*

given in tabulation form, has no special meaning, because it is difficult for him to understand these figures. Alternatively if they are exhibited in diagram/graph form they appeal to all and sundry. Side by side pictures provide comparative importance to its visitors. Therefore, each students of social research should acknowledge with the art of demonstrating figure in the form of pictures. **Prof. Bowley**[25] **(1973)** very nicely said, "Diagrams are merely an aid to eyes and a means of saving time."In this research study, the investigator demonstrated data in the form of simple diagram, multiple diagrams and Pie-diagram so that (1) Effective and attractive presentation of data may be ensured (2) Data would be simple in understanding (3) Time may be saved (4) Data can easily be compared (5) Data may be simple in one outlook (6) Proved utilization for research and they should be able to indicate about future studies.

# REFERENCES

1.  Stuart Chase,The Proper Study of Mankind, the Free Press, Glencoe, 1956, p. 6.
2.  Karl Pearson,The Grammar of Science, A and C, Black Publishing Co., London, 1951, p. 1.
3.  Festinger Learner and Daniel, Research Methods in Behavioural Science, Mac-Graw Hill Book Co., 1976, p. 30.
4.  Mukherji, R.N., Social Research and Statistics, VIII Ed. Matra Ashish Tilak Colony, Subhas Nagar, Meerut, 2001, p. 1.
5.  Young, P.V., Scientific Social Survey and Research, Asia Publication House, Bombay, 1960, p.44.
6.  Moser, C.A., Survey Methods in Social Investigation, Heinemann and Co., London, 1961, p. 3.
7.  Kerlinger, F.N.,The Foundation of Behavioural Research, Rinehart and Winston Press, Halt, New York, 1964, p. 4.
8.  Jahoda, Seltiz andDeutach Cook, Research Methods in Social  Relations, Rinehart and Winston Press, Holt, 1950, p. 357.
9.  Pearson, K.,The Grammar of Science, A and C Black Basil and Co., Landon, 1911.
10. Kapil H.K., Research methods in Behavioural Sciences, Har Prasad Bhargava and Sons, Hospital Road, Agra, 1984, p. 37.
11. Arnold Brachet (et.al.), Research Methods in Social Sciences, Mc Graw Hill Book Co., New York, 1970, p.12.
12. Jahoda, Seltiz Deutach Cook, Research Methods in Social Relations, Rinehart and Winston Press, Holt, New York, 1950, p.33.
13. Bajpai, R.K. and Mishra J.P., Formulation of Research Design, All India Conference on Research Design in Social Sciences, Paper Presented on 22nd& 23rd Feb., 1991 (conducted by Dr. B.S. Govt. (P.G.) College Gwalior, with the collaboration of Higher Education Deptt. of M.P. Govt.).

14. Petter I.R. and Others,Sociology, inquiring into Society, Second Edition, St. Martin Press, New York, 1982, p.2.

15. Young P.V.,Scientific Social survey and research, Asia Publishing House, Bombay, 1960, p.127.

16. Moser C.A. and Kalton C.,Survey Methods in Social investigation, Mc-Graw Hill Book Co., 1960, p. 271.

17. Robert E. Chaddock,Principles and methods of statistics, Miffin Publishing Co., Boston, 1995, p. 43.

18. Conner, I.R.,Statistics in theory and practice, Asia Publishing House, Bombay, 1966, p.18.

19. Jahoda S. and Cook D.,Research Methods in Social Relations, Rinehart and Winston Press, Holt, 1960, p. 270.

20. Ghose M.K. and Choudhary S.C.,Statistics: Theory and Practice, Vivek Prakashan, Delhi, 1960, p. 94.

21. Young P.V.;Scientific Social Surveys and research, Prentice Hall of India (Pvt. Ltd.), New Delhi, 1960, p. 509.

22. Young P.V.;Scientific Social Survey and Research, 1960, p.509.

23. Young P.V.;Scientific Social Survey and Research 1960, p.509.

24. Boddmgton D. Robert;Statistics and its application to commerce, Miffin Pub. Co., Boston, 1961, p. 140.

25. Bowley C.H.;Research Methodology, Deep and Deep Publications, New Delhi, 1973, p. 188.

26. Goode W.J. and Hatt P.K.;Research Method in Social Relations, Rinehart and Winston Press Holt, New York, 1963, p. 50.

27. Petter H. Mann;Methods of Sociological enquiry, Black Well, Basil, Oxford, 1956, p. 551.

28. Joheda C.S. (et.al.) ; Research Method in Social Relations, Rinehart and Winston Press, Holt, New York, 1963, p. 50.

29. Young P.V.; Scientific Social Surveys and Research, Prentice Hall of India (Pvt. Ltd.), New Delhi, 1975, p. 131.

30. Petter H. Mann; Methods of Sociological Enquiry; Basin Blackwell Publishing Co. and Distributors, Oxford, 1968, p. 38-39.

❖❖❖❖❖

# CHAPTER 3
# Socio-Economic and Cultural Background of Respondents

The socio-economic and cultural conditions of the respondents play an important role especially in Social studies, because it is necessary and essential to understand the major variables used under study. **Muthaiya[1] (2003)** has stated that, 'the variables play an important role to draw logical conclusions regarding the study problem', because social problems occur due to the cause-effect relationship. Here in this chapter, the researcher has studied the socio-demographic profile of the women respondents selected for the study purpose. Therefore, first of all it is necessary to understand the meaning and the concept of the word 'family'. Sociologist **MacIver and Page[2] (1956:243)** have stated that, 'Family is the first and most important institution of the society around which the whole society revolves'. No society or any part of the society can ignore the paramount importance and significance of this social institution. Each and every social animal is closely related to this institution. That's why, it is said that the family for children is a cradle, for youth is garden and for old-age it is the hospital or shelter. It is the family which plays a vital role for the continuity and existence of the society.

The word 'Family' is derived from the Latin word 'Famulus' which means 'Servant' or 'to serve', i.e. who serves or provide services. Many sociologists have defined family by stressing on various points given as under. According to **Anderson & Parker[3] (1960:15)**, the family has two forms as: (i) Family of orientation and (ii) Family of procreation. Though it is also said that, "Culture is the man-made part of the environment[4]. It is clear that all human products are the part of human culture and all these products affect the society. To study socio-cultural[5] and social-demographic aspects of any community or group, it is essential to study the various aspects which are known as continuant. Unit of the structures of the said aspects, such as: age, sex, caste, religion, educational status, marital status, type of family, family size, occupation of family, income of family, expenditure of family, living conditions, socio economic status of family, beliefs traditions etc. so the researcher has classified the related variables into two major parts (i) dependent variables and (ii) independent variables for study.

As we know that the family has two norms: (a) Family of orientation (b) Family of procreation, Sociologists like Kingsley Devis[6] (1977:80), Burgess E.W.[7] (The Family, 1953:8) and MacIver and Page[8] (Society, 1959:243) have defined family well. In other words, the family is a more or less durable association of husband and wife with or without children, but in this study the couple(s) with one or more living children, and wife not exceeding 49 years of age at the time of survey have been selected for study purpose. As a matter of fact an Indian family has the characteristics as, common habitation, common wealth, common kitchen, worship and requirements, to the fulfillment of various activities and functions. Besides all these merits, it is also notable characteristic that the supremacy of the family head is out of question. In this reference the foregoing matter has focus on the socio-demographic profile of the Muslim couple(s) respondents selected for the investigation purpose. The following table no. 3(1) shows the sex-wise distribution of 300 surveyed Muslim couples:

Table No. 3(1): Sexwise distribution of 300 couple respondents

| S.No. | Sex of respondents | Frequencies | Percentage |
|-------|--------------------|-------------|------------|
| 1 | Male (Husband) | 300 | 50.00 |
| 2 | Female (Wife) | 300 | 50.00 |
|  | **Total** | **600** | **100.00** |

It is clear from the above table no. 3(1) that amongst 300 selected Muslim couples there are 300(50%) male and 300(50%) female respondents, who are living as husband and wife in their families. The following table no. 3(2) focuses on the age groups (in years) of 300 Muslim couple respondents selected for the study purpose:

Table No. 3(2): Age-structure of Muslim couple respondents

| S.No. | Age Group (in years) | No. of Couples | Percentage |
|-------|----------------------|----------------|------------|
| 1 | Below 20 yrs. | 03 | 01.00 |
| 2 | 20 – 24 | 10 | 03.33 |
| 3 | 24 – 28 | 28 | 09.33 |
| 4 | 28 – 32 | 52 | 17.34 |
| 5 | 32 – 36 | 90 | 30.00 |
| 6 | 36 – 40 | 91 | 30.33 |
| 7 | 40 – 44 | 20 | 06.67 |
| 8 | Above 44 yrs. | 06 | 02.00 |
|  | **Total** | **300** | **100.00** |

It is clear from the above table that amongst 300 couples; 3(1%) couples are of the age below 20 years, 10(3.33%) couples 20 to 24 years of age, 28(9.33%) couples 24 to 28 years of age, 52(17.34%) couples 28 to 32 years of age, 90(30%) couples 32 to 36 years of age, 91(30.33%) couples 36 to 40 years of age, 20(6.67%) couples 40 to 44 years of age, and only 6(2%) couples are found above than 44 years of age. It is clear from the analysis of data that all the 300 couples are selected of specific age group i.e. 15 to 49 years of age. The following table no. 3(3) shows the type of families of the 300 surveyed couples:

**Table No. 3(3): Type of Surveyed families of the Muslim couples**

| S.No. | Type of surveyed families | Frequencies | Percentage |
|-------|---------------------------|-------------|------------|
| 1 | Nuclear families | 120 | 40.00 |
| 2 | Joint families | 163 | 54.33 |
| 3 | Extended families | 17 | 05.67 |
| | **Total** | **300** | **100.00** |

The above table shows that amongst 300 surveyed families 120 (40%) families are nuclear, 163(54.33%) joint and 17(5.67%) extended. It is clear from the data that amongst the surveyed families, the joint families are in majority. The following table no. 3(4) reveals the distribution of number of family members in the families of surveyed couples:

**Table No. 3(4): Number of family members in surveyed couple's families**

| S.No. | Number of Family members | Frequencies of couples | Percentage |
|-------|--------------------------|------------------------|------------|
| 1 | less than 3 | 20 | 06.67 |
| 2 | 3 – 5 | 26 | 08.66 |
| 3 | 5 – 7 | 34 | 11.33 |
| 4 | 7 – 9 | 60 | 20.00 |
| 5 | 9 – 11 | 71 | 23.67 |
| 6 | more than 11 | 89 | 29.67 |
| | **Total** | **300** | **100.00** |
| The average number of family members $\Sigma fx/N = 2356/300 = 7.85$ | | | |

The present table depicts that amongst the 300 surveyed Muslim couples, 20(6.67) couples families have less than 3 members, 26 (8.66%) 3 to 5 members, 34(11.33%) 5 to 7 members, 60(20%) 7 to 9 members, 71(23.67%) 9 to 11 members and 89(29.67%) couple's families have more than 11 members in their families. The investigator has also calculated the average number of family members/family and found 7.85 i.e. 8

members/family, which is much more today. The following table no. 3(5) shows the sexwise distribution of the family members in 300 surveyed Muslim families:

**Table No. 3(5): Sexwise distribution of the family members in surveyed families**

| S.No. | Sexwise distribution (Male & Female) | No. of Families | % |
|---|---|---|---|
| 1 | 1 male & 1 female | 06 | 02.00 |
| 2 | 2 males & 1 female | 12 | 04.00 |
| 3 | 1 male & 2 females | 12 | 04.00 |
| 4 | 2 males & 2 females | 29 | 09.67 |
| 5 | 3 males & 1 female | 30 | 10.00 |
| 6 | 1 male & 3 females | 15 | 05.00 |
| 7 | 3 males & 2 females | 28 | 09.33 |
| 8 | 2 males & 3 females | 08 | 02.67 |
| 9 | 3 males & 3 females | 18 | 06.00 |
| 10 | 4 males & 1 female | 06 | 02.00 |
| 11 | 1 male & 4 females | 14 | 04.67 |
| 12 | 4 males & 2 females | 34 | 11.33 |
| 13 | 2 males & 4 females | 18 | 06.00 |
| 14 | 4 males & 3 females | 24 | 08.00 |
| 15 | 3 males & 4 females | 17 | 05.67 |
| 16 | 5 males & 3 females | 13 | 04.33 |
| 17 | 3 males & 5 females | 05 | 01.66 |
| 18 | 6 males & 2 females | 11 | 03.67 |
| | Total | 300 | 100.00 |

It is clear from the analysis of the data of above table that amongst 300 families; 6(2%) surveyed families have one male and one female, 12(4%) families 2 males & 1 female, 12(4%) families 1 male & 2 females, 29(9.67%) families 2 males & 2 females, 30(15%) families 3 males & 1 female, 15(5%) families 1 males & 3 females, 28(9.33%)families 3 males & 2 females, 8(2.67%)families 2 males & 3 females, 18(6%)families 3 males & 3 females, 6(2%)families 4 males & 1 female, 14(4.67%)families 1 male & 4 females, 34(11.33%)families 4 males & 2 females, 18(6%)families 2 males & 4 females, 24(8%)families 4 males & 3 females, 17(5.67%)families 3 males & 4 females, 13(4.33%)families 5 males & 3 females, 5(1.66%)families 3 males & 5 females and 11(3.67%)families 6 males & 2 females. The following table no. 3(6) shows the family structure of 300 surveyed Muslim families:

### Table No. 3(6): The Family Structure of Surveyed Muslim Families

| S. No. | Family Members in the Family | No. of Families | % |
|--------|------------------------------|-----------------|------|
| 1 | Husband & Wife | 06 | 02.00 |
| 2 | Husband, Wife & unmarried children | 198 | 66.00 |
| 3 | Husband, Wife & husband's Brother | 18 | 06.00 |
| 4 | Husband, Wife & mother-in-law | 12 | 04.00 |
| 5 | Husband, Wife, Children & grandfather | 12 | 04.00 |
| 6 | Husband, Wife, Children & grandmother | 24 | 08.00 |
| 7 | Husband, Wife, Children & grandfather/mother | 12 | 04.00 |
| 8 | Husband, Wife, Children & brother of grand father & mother | 06 | 02.00 |
| 9 | Husband, Wife, Children &Husband's sister & brother | 04 | 01.33 |
| 10 | Husband, Wife, Children & others | 08 | 02.67 |
| | Total | 300 | 100.00 |

The present table shows the distribution of family members in 300 surveyed families. The following table no. 3(7) focuses on the distribution of the family members (Adult & Children per family) among 300 surveyed Muslim couple's families:

## Table No. 3(7): The distribution of family members among the surveyed Muslim couple's families

| S.No. | Family members in all | | Frequencies of Couple's families | Percentage |
|---|---|---|---|---|
| | Adult | Children | | |
| 1 | 2 | -- | 06 | 02.00 |
| 2 | 2 | 1 | 06 | 02.00 |
| 3 | 2 | 2 | 36 | 12.00 |
| 4 | 3 | 2 | 18 | 06.00 |
| 5 | 2 | 3 | 24 | 08.00 |
| 6 | 3 | -- | 18 | 06.00 |
| 7 | 3 | 1 | 12 | 04.00 |
| 8 | 3 | 3 | 12 | 04.00 |
| 9 | 4 | -- | 36 | 12.00 |
| 10 | 4 | 1 | 06 | 02.00 |
| 11 | 4 | 2 | 12 | 04.00 |
| 12 | 2 | 4 | 30 | 10.00 |
| 13 | 4 | 3 | 24 | 08.00 |
| 14 | 5 | 2 | 18 | 06.00 |
| 15 | 2 | 5 | 06 | 02.00 |
| 16 | 5 | 3 | 06 | 02.00 |
| 17 | 6 | -- | 06 | 02.00 |
| 18 | 6 | 1 | 06 | 02.00 |
| 19 | 6 | 2 | 12 | 04.00 |
| 20 | 6 | more than 5 | 06 | 02.00 |
| | | Total | 300 | 100.00 |

The analysis of the data of the above table no. 3(7) shows that amongst 300 surveyed couple's families; 6(2%) families have 2 adults but no child, 6(2%) families 2 adults and 1 child, 36(12%) families 2 adults and 2 children, 18(6%) families 3 adults and 2 children, 24(8%) families 2 adults and 3 children, 18(6%) families 3 adults but no child, 12(4%) families 3 adults and 1 child, 12(4%) families 3 adults and 3 children's, 36(12%) families 4 adults but no child, 6(2%) families 4 adults and one child, 12(4%) families 4 adults and 2 children, 30(10%) families 2 adults and 4 children, 24(8%) families 4 adults and 3 children, 18(6%) families 5 adults and 2 children, 6(2%) families 2 adults and 5 children, 6(2%) families 5 adults and 3 children, 6(2%) families 6 adults but no child, 6(2%) families 6 adults and 1 child, 12(4%) families 6 adults and 2 children, and 6(2%) couple's families have 6 adults and 5 & more than 5 children. The following table no. 3(8) shows the distribution of the number of children on 300 surveyed Muslim couples:

**Table No. 3(8): The distribution of children on the surveyed couples**

| S. No. | Number of Children | No. of Couples | Percentage |
|--------|--------------------|----------------|------------|
| 1 | No issue/child (but pregnant) | 04 | 01.33 |
| 2 | 1 | 11 | 03.67 |
| 3 | 2 | 19 | 06.33 |
| 4 | 3 | 21 | 07.00 |
| 5 | 4 | 42 | 14.00 |
| 6 | 5 | 48 | 16.00 |
| 7 | 6 | 30 | 10.00 |
| 8 | 7 | 75 | 25.00 |
| 9 | 8 | 15 | 05.00 |
| 10 | 9 | 08 | 02.67 |
| 11 | 10 | 26 | 08.67 |
| 12 | 10 and above | 01 | 00.33 |
| | Total | 300 | 100.00 |
| Total number of children per surveyed Muslim couple; calculated by the formula : $\Sigma fx/N = 1688/300 = 5.63 = 6$ (approx) children/couple | | | |

The above table 3(8) shows that amongst the 300 surveyed Muslim couples, each couple has six children (approximately) at the time of field survey; which are much more today. [Please, see table no. 3(4) for the total number of the family members per surveyed family which were found at the time of survey]. The researcher has found (at the time of survey) that there is lack of proper accommodation for the living and food facilities for the family members due to the ill economic conditions and population pressure. It has also seen at the time of survey; that they are hand to mouth always.

The following table no. 3(9) focuses on the housing conditions of the 300 surveyed Muslim couples:

**Table No. 3(9): Housing conditions of Respondent couples**

| S. No. | Types of House/ Housing Conditions | No. of Couples | Percentage |
|---|---|---|---|
| 1 | Kachche | 57 | 19.00 |
| 2 | Pakke | 28 | 09.33 |
| 3 | Kachche-Pakke | 215 | 71.67 |
| | Total | 300 | 100.00 |

It is clear from the above table no. 3(9) that amongst 300 surveyed respondent couples; 57(19%) couples are residing in Kachche houses, only 28(9.33%) couples in Pakke houses and maximum 215(71.67%) couples are residing in Kachche-pakke houses. The foregoing table depicts on the accommodation and habitation conditions of the respondents:

**Table No. 3(10): Number of Rooms, Accommodation & Residential conditions of the respondent couples**

| S. No. | No. of rooms in houses | Frequencies of couple's families | Residential conditions (frequencies & percentage) | | | |
|---|---|---|---|---|---|---|
| | | | Kitchen | Bathroom | Latrine | Kitchen garden |
| 1 | One | 154 (51.33) | -- (00.00) | -- (00.00) | -- (00.00) | -- (00.00) |
| 2 | Two | 69 (23.00) | 02 (00.66) | 06 (02.00) | 02 (00.67) | -- (00.00) |
| 3 | Three | 55 (18.33) | 26 (08.67) | 08 (02.67) | 09 (03.00) | -- (00.00) |
| 4 | Four | 14 (04.67) | 39 (09.67) | 10 (03.33) | 42 (14.00) | 01 (00.33) |
| 5 | Five | 08 (02.67) | 33 (11.00) | 20 (06.67) | 45 (15.00) | 01 (00.33) |
| | Total (%) | 300 (100.00) | 90 (30.00) | 44 (14.67) | 98 (32.67) | 02 (00.67) |

(Percentages have been given in the parentheses)

The analysis of the data of the above table no. 3(10) clarifies that amongst 300 respondent couple's families; 154(51.33%) families are residing in one room without any kind of facilities of kitchen, bathroom and latrine, 69(23%) having two rooms, 55(18.33%) couples have three rooms (having 8.67% kitchen, 2.67% bathroom, 0.67% latrine) and only 22(7.33%) respondent couple's families are living within four to five rooms having facilities of kitchen, bathroom and latrine etc. The question was asked to all the 300 respondents, "Are you satisfied with your housing and living conditions?" The responses given by the respondents are shown in the following table no. 3(11):

**Table No. 3(11): Attitudes of the respondents towards their housing & living conditions: According to Thurston attitude scale**

| S. No. | Attitudes of the respondents | No. of couples | No. of respondents | % |
|--------|------------------------------|----------------|--------------------|----|
| 1 | Satisfied | 37 | 74 | 12.33 |
| 2 | Neutral | 75 | 150 | 25.00 |
| 3 | Dis-satisfied | 188 | 376 | 62.67 |
| | Total | 300 | 600 | 100.00 |

It is clear from the above table that amongst 600 respondents (300 husbands and 300 wives); 74(12.33%) respondents are found satisfied with their housing and living conditions, 150(25%) answered neutral and 376(62.67%) are dissatisfied. The following table no. 3(12) depicts the attitudes of all the respondents regarding their housing and living conditions according to Likert's attitude scale:

**Table No. 3(12): Attitudes of respondents regarding their housing & living conditions according to Likert attitude scale**

| S. No. | Attitudes of the respondents | No. of couples | No. of respondents | Percentage |
|--------|------------------------------|----------------|--------------------|------------|
| 1 | Fully satisfied | 06 | 12 ⎫ 74 | 02.00 ⎫ 12.33 |
| 2 | Less satisfied | 31 | 62 ⎭ | 10.33 ⎭ |
| 3 | Neutral | 75 | 150 | 25.00 |
| 4 | Less dissatisfied | 70 | 140 ⎫ 376 | 23.33 ⎫ 62.67 |
| 5 | Fully dissatisfied | 118 | 236 ⎭ | 39.34 ⎭ |
| | Total | 300 | 600 | 100.00 |

The above table 3(12) depicts that amongst 300 sampled couples; only 6(2%) couples are found fully satisfied with their housing and living conditions while; 31(10.33%) couples are found less satisfied, 75(25%) couples neutral, 70(23.33%) couples less dis-satisfied and 118(39.34%) couples fully dis-satisfied. But it is noteworthy that 376(62.67%) couple respondents are dissatisfied with their housing and living conditions.

Undoubtedly; caste and caste stratification (hierarchy) play an important role in society. Even in Muslims like Hindus, the investigator has found caste categories i.e. General, Backward and SC/STs. The following table no. 3(13) shows the distribution of the caste structure of 300 surveyed Muslim couple respondents.

**Table No. 3(13): The distribution of Muslim couple respondents according to the Caste Categories**

| S. No. | Caste Categories | Frequencies | Percentage |
|--------|-----------------|-------------|------------|
| 1 | General | 202 | 67.34 |
| 2 | Backward | 40 | 13.33 |
| 3 | SC & STs | (51+07) | 19.33 |
| | **Total** | **300** | **100.00** |

The above table no. 3(13) reveals that amongst 300 sampled Muslim couples; 202(67.34%) couples are of the general category, 40(13.33%) backward, 51(17%) scheduled castes and only 7(2.33%) are of the scheduled Tribes. It is noteworthy that Muslim couples of the general categories are found in majority in the universe. The following table 3(14) focuses on the caste and sub caste structure of the surveyed 300 Muslim couple respondents; with respect to their frequencies and percentage:

Table No. 3(14): Caste structure of the couple respondents

| S. No. | Caste and sub caste Categories | Frequencies & Percentage of couples | Total Percentage |
|--------|-------------------------------|-------------------------------------|------------------|
| 1 | General : Sheikh | 34(11.33) | 202 (67.34) |
|   | Sayeed | 61(20.34) | |
|   | Mughal | 59(19.67) | |
|   | Pathan | 48(16.00) | |
| 2 | Backward :Nai | 05(01.67) | 40 (13.33) |
|   | Fakeer | 10(03.33) | |
|   | Ansari | 13(04.33) | |
|   | Darzi | 10(03.33) | |
|   | Teli | 02(00.67) | |
| 3 | Scheduled :Dhobi | 13(04.33) | 51 (17.00) |
|   | Qureshi | 25(08.33) | |
|   | Kasai | 03(01.00) | |
|   | Bhisti | 10(03.33) | |

(The figures shown in parenthesis are percentage)

The above table no. 3(14) shows that amongst 300 surveyed Muslim couples; 202(67.34%) couples are of General castes, 40 (13.33%) couples are of Backward castes; 51(17%) couples are of scheduled castes and only 7(2.33%) couples are of STs; have selected for the investigation.

The following table no. 3(15) shows the attitudes of the 300 couples i.e. 600 Muslim respondents regarding their married life:

Table No. 3(15): The attitudes of respondents regarding their
married life; according to 'Thurston' attitude scale

| S. No. | Attitudes of Respondents | Frequencies | Percentage |
|--------|--------------------------|-------------|------------|
| 1 | Satisfied | 300 | 50.00 |
| 2 | Dis-satisfied | 212 | 35.33 |
| 3 | Neutral | 88 | 14.67 |
| | Total | 600 | 100.00 |

The attitudes of 600 Muslim respondents regarding their married life: The scaling is giving according to 'Likert' attitude scale:

| S. No. | Attitudes of the Respondents | Partially | Fully | Neutral | Total |
|--------|------------------------------|-----------|-------|---------|-------|
| 1 | Satisfied | 98(16.33) | 202(33.67) | --(00.00) | 300(50.00) |
| 2 | Dis-satisfied | 100(16.67) | 112(18.67) | --(00.00) | 212(35.33) |
| 3 | Neutral | --(00.00) | --(00.00) | 88(14.67) | 88(14.67) |
| | | | | G. Total | 600(100.00) |

It is clear from the analysis of the data of the above table no. 3(15) that amongst 600 Muslim respondents; 98(16.33%) are partially satisfied, 202(33.67%) fully satisfied, while 100(16.67%) respondents are partially dissatisfied and 112(18.67%) fully dissatisfied; but 88(14.67%) respondents said un-decided. The following table no. 3(16) shows the opinions of the respondents regarding their standard of living:

Table No. 3(16): The opinion of respondents regarding their
Level of standard of living

| S. No. | Level of Standard of Living | Frequencies | Percentage |
|--------|------------------------------|-------------|------------|
| 1 | Low | 480 | 80.00 |
| 2 | Medium | 72 | 12.00 |
| 3 | High | 48 | 08.00 |
| | Total | 600 | 100.00 |

The table no. 3(16) depicts that amongst 600 respondents; 480(80%) respondents have opined low, 72(12%) opined medium and only 48(8%) respondents opined high level of their standard of living. In the light of above facts and figures it may be concluding that more than 3/4 of the respondents are living low level of life. The following table no. 3(17) shows the sexwise distribution of the educational status of the respondents:

## Table No. 3(17): Sexwise distribution of Educational status
### of the respondents

| S. No. | Educational Status | Sexwise frequencies of the respondents | | Total |
|---|---|---|---|---|
| | | Husbands | Wives | |
| 1 | Illiterate | 109(36.33) | 182(60.67) | 291(48.50) |
| 2 | Literate | 31(10.33) | 28(09.33) | 59(09.83) |
| 3 | Primary&J.H.School | 62(20.67) | 53(17.67) | 115(19.18) |
| 4 | Madhyamic & Inter | 76(25.34) | 25(08.33) | 101(16.83) |
| 5 | Graduate | 16(05.33) | 07(02.34) | 23(03.83) |
| 6 | Post Graduate | 05(01.67) | 01(00.33) | 06(01.00) |
| 7 | Others | 01(00.33) | 04(01.33) | 05(00.83) |
| | Total/Percentage | 300(50.00) | 300(50.00) | 600(100.00) |
| | (%) | (100.00) | (100.00) | (100.00) |

The above table no. 3(17) shows the sexwise distribution of educational status of respondents. Amongst 300 husbands; 109 (36.33%) husbands are illiterate, 31(10.33%) Literate, 62(20.67%) primary and junior high school, 76(25.34%) Madhyamic and Inter, 16(5.33%) Graduates, 5(1.67%) Post graduates and only 1(0.33%) have got other educations, while among 300 Wives; 182(60.67%) are illiterate, 28(9.33%) literate, 53(17.67%) primary and Junior high school, 25 (8.33%) Madhyamic and Inter, 07(02.34%) Graduates, 1(0.33%) post graduate and only 4(1.33%) have got other educations. It is clear from the above figures that the educational level of couples is very low. The following table 3(18) shows the distribution of the food habits of the respondent couples:

## Table No. 3(18): Food habits of the respondents/Couples

| S. No. | Food habits of the respondents | Frequencies of respondents | | Total |
|---|---|---|---|---|
| | | Male | Female | |
| 1 | Vegetarian | 250(41.6) | 268(44.66) | 518(86.33) |
| 2 | Vegetarian & Non-vegetarian (both) | 50(08.33) | 32(05.34) | 82(13.67) |
| | Total | 300(50.00) | 300(50.00) | 600(100.00) |

It is clear from the analysis of the data of the above table that amongst 600 respondents; 518(86.33%) respondents are vegetarian and only 82(13.67%) respondents are vegetarian and non-vegetarian both. In the light of the above findings it may be concluded that more than 3/4 respondents are vegetarian. A question was asked again to all the respondents; "Why are you vegetarian being a Muslim?" 92% of the respondents answered; "we are poor economically, while non-vegetarian food becomes costly in comparison to vegetarian food; we any how are nourishing and act of bearing the children."

To study any social problem, it is essential to study the occupational structure of the concerning units because the (main and subsidiary) occupations becomes the means of livelihood to them and for their families. The investigator has also studied the occupations of the surveyed 300 families of the sampled couples. The following table no. 3(19) focuses on the occupational structure of all the 300 respondent couples:

Table No. 3(19): The occupational structure of the respondent couples' families

| S. No. | Occupations | Frequencies | Percentage |
|--------|-------------|-------------|------------|
| 1 | Agriculture | 200 | 66.67 |
| 2 | Labour | 52 | 17.33 |
| 3 | Service | 18 | 06.00 |
| 4 | Shop keeping | 09 | 03.00 |
| 5 | Other | 21 | 07.00 |
| | **Total** | **300** | **100.00** |

The figures of the above Table no. 3(19) shows that, among 300 surveyed Muslim families of the couples; 200(66.67%) families are engaged in Agriculture, 52(17.33%) in Labour, 18(6%) in service, 9(3%) in shop keeping and 21(7%) in other occupations. The following table 3(20) shows the distribution of occupations on the basis of main and subsidiary:

## Table No. 3(20): The distribution of respondent's occupations on the basis of main and subsidiary

| S. No. | Occupations | Distribution of Occupations according to couple's frequencies | | | | | Total (%) |
|---|---|---|---|---|---|---|---|
| | | Agriculture | Labour | Service | Shopkeepingg | Other | |
| 1 | Main | 167 (55.67) | 38 (12.67) | 13 (04.33) | 06 (02.00) | 13 (04.33) | 237 (79.00) |
| 2 | Subsidiary | 33 (11.00) | 14 (04.66) | 05 (01.67) | 03 (01.00) | 08 (02.67) | 63 (21.00) |
| | Total (%) | 200 (66.67) | 52 (17.33) | 18 (06.00) | 09 (03.00) | 21 (07.00) | 300 (100.00) |

The data of this table shows that amongst 300 couples selected for the study, 237(79%) are engaged in main occupations while 63(21%) in various subsidiary occupations. Amongst 237(79%) couples who are engaged in main occupations; 167(55.67%) in Agriculture, 38 (12.67%) are engaged in Labour, 13(4.33%) in services, 6(2%) in shop keeping and 13(4.33%) in other occupations; while amongst 63(21%) families which are engaged in subsidiary occupations; 33(11%) are doing agriculture, 14(4.67%) Labour, 5(1.67%) services, 3(1%) shop keeping and remaining 8(2.67%) couples are doing other works for livelihood. The foregoing table 3(21) shows the distribution of monthly income (in Rs.) of the surveyed 300 couple's families:

**Table No.3 (21): Monthly income of surveyed couple's families (in Rs.)**

| S. No. | Monthly Income (in Rs.) | Frequencies | % |
|--------|-------------------------|-------------|------|
| 1 | below 500 | 06 | 02.00 |
| 2 | 500 – 1000 | 36 | 12.00 |
| 3 | 1000 – 1500 | 40 | 13.33 |
| 4 | 1500 – 2000 | 58 | 19.33 |
| 5 | 2000 – 2500 | 72 | 24.00 |
| 6 | 2500 – 3000 | 24 | 08.00 |
| 7 | 3000 – 3500 | 20 | 06.67 |
| 8 | 3500 – 4000 | 18 | 06.00 |
| 9 | 4000 – 4500 | 12 | 04.00 |
| 10 | 4500 – 5000 | 09 | 03.00 |
| 11 | more than 5000 | 05 | 01.67 |
| | **Total** | **300** | **100.00** |
| From the formula; $\Sigma fx/N$, Average monthly income/family Rs. 2201.00 | | | |

It is clear from the above table no. 3(21) that amongst 300 surveyed couple's families; the monthly income of 6(2%) families is below Rs. 500/-, 36(12%) families between 500 to 1000 Rs., 98(32.66%) families between 1000 to 2000 Rs., 96(32%) families between 2000 to 3000 Rs., 38(12.67%) families between 3000 to 4000 Rs., 21(7%) families between 4000 to 5000 Rs., but only 5(1.67%) families have monthly income more than Rs. 5000. The researcher has calculated average monthly income per family Rs. 2201.00 by the formula of mean $\Sigma fx/N$.

It is essential to know the monthly expenditure and family budget to assess/evaluate the economic conditions of any family. Therefore the investigator has also calculated the monthly expenditure (in Rs.) of the surveyed families given as under in table no. 3(22):

Table No. 3(22): Monthly expenditure of surveyed families (in Rs.)

| S. No. | Monthly Expenditure (in Rs.) | Frequencies | Percentage |
|--------|------------------------------|-------------|------------|
| 1 | 500 – 1000 | 10 | 03.33 |
| 2 | 1000 – 1500 | 17 | 05.67 |
| 3 | 1500 – 2000 | 20 | 06.67 |
| 4 | 2000 – 2500 | 75 | 25.00 |
| 5 | 2500 – 3000 | 98 | 32.67 |
| 6 | 3000 – 3500 | 40 | 13.33 |
| 7 | 3500 – 4000 | 38 | 12.66 |
| 8 | more than 4000 | 02 | 00.67 |
|  | **Total** | **300** | **100.00** |

The table no. 3(22) depicts that amongst 300 surveyed families; the monthly expenditure of 10(3.33%) families is between Rs. 500 to 1000, 17(5.67%) families between Rs. 1000-1500, 20(6.67%) families between Rs. 1500-2000, 75(25%) families between Rs. 2000-2500, 98(32.67%) families between Rs. 2500-3000, 40(13.33%) families between Rs. 3000-3500, 38(12.66%) families between Rs. 3500-4000 and only 2(0.67%) families have expense more than 4000 Rs. per month. By statistically on an average the monthly expenditure of respondent's families is found Rs. 2609.33* per surveyed Muslim family.

Because the average expenditure per surveyed family (Rs. 2609.33) is more than the average income per surveyed family (Rs. 2201). Hence, it is clear that the Muslim families are hand to mouth and living in distress and indebtedness. The following table no. 3(23) focuses on debt and borrow (in Rs.) on the surveyed Muslim families.

Table No. 3(23): Debt and Borrow (in Rs.) on the surveyed Muslim families

| S. No. | Debt & Borrowness (in Rs.) | Frequencies | % |
|--------|----------------------------|-------------|------|
| 1 | -- | 16 | 05.33 |
| 2 | below 100 | 109 | 36.33 |
| 3 | 100 - 200 | 76 | 25.33 |
| 4 | 200 - 300 | 58 | 19.34 |
| 5 | 300 - 400 | 17 | 05.67 |
| 6 | 400 - 500 | 10 | 03.33 |
| 7 | 500 - 600 | 08 | 02.67 |
| 8 | above 6000 | 06 | 02.00 |
| | Total | 300 | 100.00 |
| Average Debtness/Borrowness $\Sigma fx/N = 50100/300 = 167$ Rs./Family* | | | |

It is clear from the statistical calculation that on an average per surveyed family is in debt from Rs. 167/- while only 16(5.33%) negligible families are not in debt/borrow. The following table no. 3(24) focuses on the variables taken under study at a glance:

# Table No. 3(24) : Variables : At a Glance, used under study

| | | | | | | | |
|---|---|---|---|---|---|---|---|
| 1 | Age Group (in yrs) | below 20 yrs 03(01.00) | 20-28 38(12.67) | 28-36 142(47.33) | 36-44 111(37.00) | 44 & above 06(02.00) | Total 300(100.00) |
| 2 | Education | Illiterate+Lit. 140(46.67) | Primary+J.H.Sc. 138(46.00) | Madhyamic 76(25.33) | Graduate 16(05.33) | P.G.+Others 06(02.00) | Total 300(100.00) |
| 3 | Family structure | Nuclear 120(40.00) | Joint 163(54.33) | Extended 17(05.67) | -- 00(00.00) | -- 00(00.00) | Total 300(100.00) |
| 4 | Caste category | General 202(67.34) | Backward 40(13.33) | Scheduled 51(17.00) | Sc. Tribe 07(02.33) | 00(00.00) | Total 300(100.00) |
| 5 | Occupations | Agriculture 200(66.67) | Labour 52(17.33) | Service 18(06.00) | Shopkeeing 09(03.00) | Other 21(07.00) | Total 300(100.00) |
| 6 | No. of family members | less than 3 20(06.67) | 3-7 60(20.00) | 7-9 60(20.00) | 9-11 71(23.67) | more than 11 89(29.67) | Total 300(100.00) |
| 7 | House Types | Kachche 57(19.00) | Pakke 28(09.33) | Kachche-Pakke 215(71.67) | -- 00(00.00) | -- 00(00.00) | Total 300(100.00) |
| 8 | Monthly income (in Rs.) | below 1000 42(14.00) | 1000-2000 98(32.67) | 2000-3000 96(32.00) | 3000-4000 38(12.67) | 4000 & above 26(08.67) | Total 300(100.00) |
| 9 | Monthly Expenditure (in Rs.) | below 1500 27(09.00) | 1500-2500 95(31.67) | 2500-3500 138(46.00) | 3500-4000 38(12.67) | 4000 & above 02(00.67) | Total 300(100.00) |
| 10 | Food habits | Vegetarian 250(83.73) | Non-Veget. --(00.00) | Veg.+Non Veg. 50(08.33) | -- 00(00.00) | -- 00(00.00) | Total 300(100.00) |

(Note: The figures shown in parentheses are percentage)

(Note: The figures shown in parentheses are percentage)
*The calculation of average expenditure has done on the basis of formula m = A + $\Sigma$fd/N, A= Assumed mean, N = total number of surveyed families and d = deviation of mid values from assumed mean.

# REFERENCES

1.  Muthaiya R.K. ; Why the study of the profile of the respondents is essential in social problems?; A paper presented in the International Seminar, Organized by Tata Institute of Social work, Bombay on 20&21 Feb.2003.

2.  MacIver R.M. and Page C.H.; Society: Mc-Millian and Co., London, 1959, p. 243.

3.  Anderson and Parker; Society: It's Organization and Operations, 1960, p. 150.

4.  Harskovits M.J.; The Men and His works, Alfred Aknoff Publishers (Pvt. Ltd.), New York, 1956, p.17.

5.  Hans Raj; The Fundamentals of Demography (with special reference to India), Surjeet Publications, Delhi, 1978, p. 185.

6.  Kingsley Devis; Human Society; Quoted from: A New Dictionary of Sociology by Mitchel G.D., Routledge and Kegan Paul Publishers, (Pvt. Ltd.) London (II Edition), 1977, p. 80.

7.  Burgess E.W. and Lock E.B.; The Family (1953), Quoted from the above Dictionary, 1977, p. 80.

8.  Mac Iver R.M. and C.H.; Society: Mc-Millan and Co. London, 1959, page 243. Quoted from Gupta K.L. & Sharma R.P., Sociology, Surjeet Publications, Delhi, 2010, p. 107.

❖❖❖❖❖

# CHAPTER 4
# Socio-Cultural Factors and Fertility

Different surveys have revealed different rate of fertility in different religions and castes in India. The fertility among Muslims is much more than the fertility among Hindus. Different surveys have revealed this distinction. According to the Mysore Population Study, sponsored by United Nations the fertility of different religions in Banglore city was: Hindus 5.4, Muslims 5.7 and Christians 4.7. The average fertility in different religions in urban areas was found to be Hindus 5.2, Muslims 6.7 and Christians 5.5. This was further confirmed by the rural percentage of Hindus 4.8 and Muslims 5.0. These data were confirmed by other studies. According to the Survey of Kanpur by D.N. Majumdar, the fertility rate among Muslims and Hindus was 8.021 and 7.037 respectively.[1] According to the study by G.B. Saxena (1969) fertility in 3 villages of Uttar Pradesh, the fertility rate among different sections of society by caste and religion was found as follows: Muslims 6.24, Hindus 6.16. Rajputs 6.77, Artisan castes 5.50 and Bhangis and Chamars 5.43.[2] According to S.N. Agarwal's study of fertility in 6 urbanizing villages, the fertility rate among different castes was: Brahmin 7.19, Jat 7.11, Gujar and Aheer 6.97, Artisan Castes 7.16, Bhangi and Chamar 7.24. The average fertility rate for all castes was found

---

[1] Majumdar, D.N., Social Contours of an IndustrialCity, Bombay, Asia Publishing House, 1960, p. 174.

[2] Saxena, G.B., A Study of Fertility and Family Planning in 3 Villages of Uttar Pradesh, New Delhi, Institute of Economic Growth, 1969.

to be 7.08.[3] According to another study of fertility in central India, the differential fertility was as: Muslims 4.6, Hindus 4.5, Buddhists 4.9, other religions 4.1, and average for all castes 4.5.

The above studies reveal the influence of castes and religions on fertility rate. The reasons for this differential fertility, however, are not as much definite. It may be noted that Bhangis and Chamars and artisan castes have a higher fertility rate than the other castes among Hindus. However, this difference may not be so much due to caste but due to socio-economic status and illiteracy. Similar arguments may be given about the lower fertility rate among high caste Hindus. It may be more due to education and higher socio-economic status. Again, as has been already pointed out, minorities especially Muslims everywhere tend to breed fast.

"It appears to be the general opinion of Indian Demographers, who discuss the population problem of this country, that the only practical method of limiting the population is by the introduction of artificial methods of birth control, though it is not easy to exaggerate the difficulties of introducing such methods in a country where the vast majority of the people regard the propagation of male offspring as a religious duty and the reproach of barrenness as a terrible punishment for crimes committed in a former incarnation."[1]

*- Census of India (Report) 1931, Vol. I, Pt. 1.*

The Demographers and sociologists have opined that the fertility and socio-cultural factors are closely related, some affect birth rate and fertility directly and some indirectly. To get primary data in this regard, the researcher has interviewed face to face to all the 300

---

[3] Agarwal, S.N., A Demographic Study of 6 Urbanizing Villages, Bombay, Asia Publishing House, 1970, p. 101.

couples. The achieved field data will be demonstrated at proper places where required/needed.

Saxena[2] **(1989:12)** has stated that the residence and area of habitation affect the fertility indirectly. He has found in his empirical study the over population and crowd among the labours, lower sections of communities and slums. The main cause of it, is their conservative mentality. He further writes that, the habitants of slums are not found in the favour of least children but they feel more children as 'their capital' not a Burden.

In the light of above mentioned sentences, it is clear that poverty and poor sections of the society directly encourage the birth rate and fertility. On the basis of his study **Prof. Kumar (2001:207)** has also stated that urbanization and fertility are inversely proportional, while educational status and fertility level becomes also inversely proportionate. The researcher has also made efforts in this regard. The following table no. 4(1) shows the distribution of couples on the basis of the educational status.[4]

**Table No. 4(1) : The Sexwise distribution of couples on the basis of educational status:**

| S. No. | Educational Status | Sex of respondents (frequencies & %) | | Total |
|--------|--------------------|---------------------|-----------------|-------|
| | | Male (Husband) | Female (Wife) | |
| 1 | Illiterate | 16 (02.67) | 71 (11.33) | 87 (14.50) |
| 2 | Literate | 120 (20.00) | 97 (16.17) | 217 (36.17) |
| 3 | Primary & J.H.School | 65 (10.83) | 60 (10.00) | 125 (20.83) |
| 4 | Madhyamic | 62 (10.33) | 49 (08.17) | 111 (18.50) |
| 5 | Graduate | 31 (05.17) | 18 (03.00) | 49 (08.17) |
| 6 | Post Graduate | 02 (00.33) | 04 (00.67) | 06 (01.00) |
| 7 | Others | 04 (00.67) | 01 (00.16) | 05 (00.83) |
| | Total (%) | 300 (50.00) | 300 (50.00) | 600 (100.00) |

[4]Kumar Vimal; A study on 'urbanization and fertility' published article, 'Samajic Sahayog' National Research Journal, Ujjain, March and April Ank. 2001, p. 27-35.

The following table no. 4(2) shows the number of issues (children) according to the educational status of male/husbands of the surveyed female respondents:

## Table No. 4(2) : The educational Status of males & number of children:

| S. No. | Educational status of males | No. of males | Number of children who took birth | | | No. of children per 1000 males |
|---|---|---|---|---|---|---|
| | | | alive | dead | Total | |
| 1 | Illiterate | 16 | 86 | 50 | 136 | 9125 |
| 2 | Literate | 120 | 605 | 123 | 728 | 3130 |
| 3 | Primary&J.H.School | 65 | 225 | 45 | 300 | 4759 |
| 4 | Madhyamic & Inter | 62 | 234 | 32 | 266 | 4409 |
| 5 | Graduate | 31 | 97 | 04 | 101 | 3377 |
| 6 | Post-Graduate | 02 | 06 | 02 | 08 | 3190 |
| 7 | Others | 04 | 11 | 01 | 12 | 3000 |
| | Total | 300 | 1264 | 257 | 1221 | 33990 |

It is clear from the analysis of the data of the above table 4(2) that the increasing level of education is inversely proportionate to the number of children. In the light of this fact it may conclude:

(1)    The educated husbands are conscious and aware towards limited family.

(2)    Negative co-relation is found between the educational status and the number of children.

The following table no. 4(3) focuses on the number of children according to the educational status of females/wives of the surveyed male respondents:

## Table No. 4(3): The educational Status of wives & number of children:

| S. No. | Educational status of Females | No. of Females/ Wives | Number of children who took birth | | | No. of Children per 1000 females |
|---|---|---|---|---|---|---|
| | | | alive | Dead | Total | |
| 1 | Illiterate | 71 | 405 | 28 | 433 | 6220 |
| 2 | Literate | 97 | 460 | 158 | 618 | 5202 |
| 3 | Primary&J.H.School | 60 | 225 | 25 | 250 | 4700 |
| 4 | Madhyamic & Inter | 49 | 173 | 18 | 191 | 3112 |
| 5 | Graduate | 18 | 39 | 09 | 48 | 3005 |
| 6 | Post-Graduate | 04 | 02 | 01 | 03 | 2000 |
| 7 | Others | 01 | 02 | -- | 02 | 1547 |
| | Total | 300 | 1264 | 257 | 1221 | 33990 |

The table depicts that:

(1)    The increasing level of education is inversely proportional to the number of the births of the children.

(2) There is inverse co-relation between educational status and fertility rate.

(3) The total number of births per 1000 females is very high among the illiterates and literates in comparison to educated.

**Table No. 4(4): The educational status of male respondents& their mentality regarding the family size:**

| S. No. | Educational status of males | Frequencies of males | No. of alive children | Average size of family | No. of children per 1000 males |
|--------|------------------------------|----------------------|------------------------|-------------------------|--------------------------------|
| 1 | Illiterate | 16 | 86 | 5.38 | 5380 |
| 2 | Literate | 120 | 605 | 5.04 | 5040 |
| 3 | Primary&J.H.School | 65 | 225 | 3.46 | 3460 |
| 4 | Madhyamic & Inter | 62 | 234 | 3.14 | 3140 |
| 5 | Graduate | 31 | 97 | 3.13 | 3130 |
| 6 | Post-Graduate | 02 | 06 | 3.00 | 3000 |
| 7 | Others | 04 | 11 | 2.75 | 2750 |
| | Total | 300 | 1264 | 4.21 | 4210 |

It is clear from the analysis of the data of the above table 4(4) that the average size of family of illiterates is 5.38; while of the literates is found 5.04. It is also observed by the table that the educational status is increasing, but the average size of the family is decreasing. It is also clear that:

(1) The illiterates and only literates have same mentality of 5-6 children.

(2) The graduates and Post-Graduates have same mentality of 3 children i.e. these believe in limited size of family.

(3) It may be concluded that "educational status of males is inversely proportional to the average size of the family".

The following table no. 4(5) focuses on the educational status of the females and their mentality regarding the family size:

**Table No. 4(5): The educational status of females & their mentality regarding the family size:**

| S. No. | Educational status of females | Frequencies of females | No. of alive children | Average size of family | No. of children per 1000 males |
|--------|-------------------------------|------------------------|----------------------|------------------------|-------------------------------|
| 1 | Illiterate | 71 | 405 | 5.71 | 5710 |
| 2 | Literate | 97 | 460 | 4.75 | 4750 |
| 3 | Primary&J.H.School | 60 | 225 | 3.75 | 3750 |
| 4 | Madhyamic & Inter | 49 | 173 | 3.53 | 3530 |
| 5 | Graduate | 18 | 39 | 2.17 | 2170 |
| 6 | Post-Graduate | 04 | 02 | 0.50 | 500 |
| 7 | Others | 01 | 02 | 2.00 | 2000 |
| | **Total** | **300** | **1306** | **4.39** | **2240** |

The data of the above table show that the average size of families of illiterates and literates is found 5.71 and 4.75 children/female respectively, but in Graduates and post-graduate it is 2.17 and 0.5 children/female respectively which is too much less in comparison to the illiterates and only literates. It is noteworthy that the educational status of the females is inversely proportional to the average size of the family. In other words, it may be said that, "the fertility rate among the women become inversely proportional to their educational level." The reason of it is: (1) They do their marriages late, due to their education (2) They believe in minimum issues (3) If married; they use contraceptives against births or self control by celibacy. To check the fertility, the government should ban on early marriages especially at the time of getting education of girls and late marriages among girls should be encouraged.

It is seen that early marriages promote and encourage the fertility among the women. In other words, it may be said that the age of marriage play an important and significant role in fertility. Therefore the investigator has studied the effect of age of marriage on fertility among surveyed couples. The following table no. 4(6) focuses on the distribution of age at marriage of the male respondents:

## Table No. 4(6) : Distribution of age at marriage of the male respondents

| S.No. | Age of marriage (in years) | No. of males (husbands) | Percentage |
|-------|----------------------------|-------------------------|------------|
| 1 | below 15 years | 07 | 02.33 |
| 2 | 15 – 17 | 21 | 07.00 |
| 3 | 17 – 19 | 80 | 26.67 |
| 4 | 19 – 21 | 105 | 35.00 |
| 5 | 21 – 23 | 40 | 13.34 |
| 6 | 23 – 25 | 18 | 06.00 |
| 7 | 25 – 27 | 11 | 03.67 |
| 8 | 27 – 29 | 10 | 03.33 |
| 9 | 29 – 31 | 06 | 02.00 |
| 10 | 31 – 33 | 01 | 00.33 |
| 11 | 33 – 35 | 01 | 00.33 |
| 12 | 35 & above | -- | 00.00 |
| | **Total** | **300** | **100.00** |

It is clear from the analysis of the data of the above table 4(6) shows that amongst 300 male respondents; 7(2.33%) males have married below 15 years of age, 21(7%) males at 15 to 17 yrs. of age, 80 (26.67%) males at 17 to 19 yrs. of age, 105(35%) males at 19 to 21 yrs. of age, 40(13.34%) males at 21 to 23 yrs. of age, 18(6%) males at 23 to 25 yrs. of age, 11(3.67%) males at 25 to 27 yrs. of age, 10(3.33%) males at 27 to 29 yrs. of age, 6(2%) males at 29 to 31 yrs. of age, 1(0.33%) males at 31 to 33 yrs. of age and only 1(0.33%) male was married at the age of 34 yrs. no male is found, who was married at 35 yrs. of age and above it. The following table 4(7) shows the distribution of age at marriage of surveyed female respondents:

## Table No.4(7): The distribution of age at marriage of female respondents

| S.No. | Age at Marriage (in years) | No. of Females (wives) | Percentage |
|---|---|---|---|
| 1 | below 15 years | 09 | 03.00 |
| 2 | 15 – 17 | 15 | 05.00 |
| 3 | 17 – 19 | 82 | 27.33 |
| 4 | 19 – 21 | 87 | 29.00 |
| 5 | 21 – 23 | 61 | 20.33 |
| 6 | 23 – 25 | 19 | 06.33 |
| 7 | 25 – 27 | 16 | 05.34 |
| 8 | 27 – 29 | 05 | 01.67 |
| 9 | 29 – 31 | 03 | 01.00 |
| 10 | 31 – 33 | 03 | 01.00 |
| 11 | 33 – 35 | -- | 00.00 |
| 12 | 35 & above | -- | 00.00 |
| | **Total** | **300** | **100.00** |

The table no. 4(7) depicts that amongst 300 surveyed women respondents, 9(3%) have married below 15 years of age, 15(5%) females at 15 to 17 yrs. of age, 82(27.33%) females at 17 to 19 yrs. of age, 87(29%) females at 19 to 21 yrs. of age, 61(20.33%) females at 21 to 23 yrs. of age, 19(6.33%) females at 23 to 25 yrs. of age, 16(5.34%) females at 25 to 27 yrs. of age, 5(1.67%) females at 27 to 29 yrs. of age, 3(1%) males at 29 to 31 yrs. of age and remaining 3(1%) were married above the age of 31 yrs. Nobody was married at the age of 33 yrs. and above. It is clear from the table 4(6) and 4(7) that specific age at marriage of surveyed couples is 17 to 23 years. In the view of investigator it should be increased to control the fertility among the females, so that the period of fertile union is decreased. The following table shows the specific (effective) age of marriage among females and average no. of children per couple at the time of survey:

## Table No. 4(8) : The effective age of marriage among females & average no. of children/couple

| S. No. | Effective age of marriage (in years) | No. of couples | Number of children (alive) | |
|---|---|---|---|---|
| | | | Total no. of children | Average children per couple |
| 1 | below 15 years | 04 | 02 | 00.50 |
| 2 | 15 – 18 | 12 | 37 | 03.08 |
| 3 | 18 – 21 | 60 | 210 | 03.50 |
| 4 | 21 – 24 | 100 | 398 | 03.98 |
| 5 | 24 – 27 | 115 | 553 | 04.82 |
| 6 | 27 – 30 | 05 | 14 | 02.80 |
| 7 | 30 – 33 | 02 | 05 | 02.50 |
| 8 | 33 & above | 02 | 01 | 00.50 |
| | Total | 300 | 1220 | 04.67 |

At the time of survey, it was found that all the 300 surveyed couples have total 1220 children i.e. on an average 4.67 children per couple; which are much more today. In the view of investigator, those couples who are married in early age, they produce more children in comparison to those couples who married late. Therefore, they are suggested to marry late i.e. after effective age, so that the size of family may limited.

It is true, according to demographers and sociologists that the caste structure and fertility becomes closely related, because in different caste categories, the age of marriage becomes indifferent. For example, it is seen that in Backward Castes and SC/STs, the marriages of boys and girls are made in early age in comparison to the general caste categories. Hence and therefore, the fertility rate among Backwards, SC & STs are high in comparison to general castes. To know the real picture, the researcher has studied the age at marriage, specific age and age difference among the surveyed couples, structure of the respondents on the basis of sex and caste categories.

## Table No. 4(9): Age at marriage, specific age & age difference in effective age of couples, on the basis of sex and caste categories

| S. No. | Caste Categories & Sex of respondents | Class intervals (in yrs.) of age at marriage | | | | | | | | | Specific age (in years) | Difference in specific age (in year) |
|---|---|---|---|---|---|---|---|---|---|---|---|---|
| | | below 15 | 15-18 | 18-21 | 21-24 | 24-27 | 27-30 | 30-33 | above 33 | Total | | |
| 1 | General Castes: | | | | | | | | | | | |
| | (a) Male | 06 | 10 | 40 | 90 | 28 | 10 | 06 | 04 | 202 | 18-27 | |
| | (b) Female | 12 | 20 | 62 | 71 | 12 | 02 | -- | -- | 199 | 18-24 | 3-0 yrs |
| 2 | Backward Castes: | | | | | | | | | | | |
| | (a) Male | 04 | 10 | 11 | 06 | 04 | 03 | 02 | 02 | 41 | 15-21 | |
| | (b) Female | 05 | 16 | 09 | 08 | 02 | -- | -- | -- | 40 | 15-21 | 0-0 yrs |
| 3 | SCs & STs Castes: | | | | | | | | | | | |
| | (a) Male | 06 | 20 | 16 | 12 | 03 | 02 | 01 | -- | 60 | 15-24 | |
| | (b) Female | 11 | 26 | 13 | 06 | 01 | -- | -- | 01 | 58 | 15-21 | 3-0 yrs |
| | Total | 44 | 110 | 151 | 193 | 50 | 17 | 09 | 06 | 600 | -- | -- |

(The figures are collected at the time of field survey and interviews)

The analysis of the data given in the above table shows that:

(i)    In general castes, the difference in specific age of marriage in the surveyed couples is found 3.0 years, while in backward castes nil.

(ii)    In scheduled castes and scheduled tribes, the difference in specific age of marriage in the surveyed couples is also found 3.0 years.

(iii)    **It is also clear, that in SCs & STs, the marriages of the boys and girls are made in early age in comparison to General and Backward castes.**

The following table no. 4(10) shows (at a glance) the fertility rates of different castes in India, according to National sample survey report 1964-65[3]:

## Table No. 4(10): Caste categories and fertility rates

| S.No. | Surveyor | Caste Categories | Fertility Rates |
|-------|----------|------------------|-----------------|
| 1 | S.N. Agrawal | Brahmin | 7.19 |
|   |   | Jat | 7.11 |
|   |   | Goojar & Ahir | 6.97 |
|   |   | Articans | 7.18 |
|   |   | Jatavs &Balmiki | 7.24 |
| 2 | Mukherji & Singh | Hindu Castes | 3.43 |
|   |   | Muslim Castes | 5.82 |
|   |   | Christians | 3.71 |
|   |   | Sikhs | 2.80 |
| 3 | G.B. Saxena | Hindu Castes | 4.50 |
|   |   | Rajpoots | 6.16 |
|   |   | Articans | 5.50 |
|   |   | Muslims | 6.24 |
|   |   | Jatavas & Balmiki | 5.43 |

(Source: National Sample Survey Organization Report 1964-65)

The following table no. 4(11) shows the fertility rates of different religious communities residing in India, according to N.S.S.O. report 2000-01; obtained from the office of the Registrar General of India, New Delhi[4]:

## Table No. 4(11) : Different religions and fertility rates

| S.No. | Religions | Rural | Urban | Average (Fertility rate) |
|-------|-----------|-------|-------|--------------------------|
| 1 | Hindu | 3.76 | 3.10 | 3.43 |
| 2 | Muslims | 5.52 | 5.40 | 5.46 |
| 3 | Sikh | -- | 2.73 | 2.73 |
| 4 | Christians | 3.56 | 3.42 | 3.49 |

It is clear from these two tables nos. 4(10) and 4(11) that the fertility rate is decreasing slowly, due to the impact of modernization and awareness among women regarding the concept and benefits of small families. The following table no. 4(12) focuses on the birth rates and fertility rates among different caste categories as per empirical study conducted by **Mathur** (2003)[5]:

**Table No. 4(12) : Birth rate per'000 mothers & the fertility rate-2003[5]**

| S. No. | Castes Categories | No. of Mothers | Births of Children (children born in 10 yrs) | Birth Rate per'000 mothers | Fertility Rate (approx.) |
|--------|-------------------|----------------|---------------------------------------------|----------------------------|--------------------------|
| 1 | General | 70 | 285 | 470.2 | 4.70 |
| 2 | Castes | 100 | 593 | 593.4 | 5.93 |
| 3 | Backwards | 50 | 367 | 734.1 | 7.34 |
| 4 | & OBC's Scheduled Cates Muslims | 30 | 168 | 560.0 | 5.60 |

The above table's no. 4(11) and 4(12) depicts that the rate of fertility among Muslims is equal (approximately) i.e. 5.46 and 5.60. The researcher has also calculated the fertility rate on the basis of his empirical study based on 300 Muslim couples of Shikohabad city. The achieved data are shown in the following table no. 4(13):

**Table No. 4(13) : Birth rate per'000 women & the fertility rate**

| S. No. | Caste Categories of Muslims | No. of Mothers [See: table no. 3(14)] | Births of Children (children born in 10 yrs) | Birth Rate per'000 mothers | Fertility Rate (approx.) |
|--------|-----------------------------|---------------------------------------|---------------------------------------------|----------------------------|--------------------------|
| 1 | General Castes | 202 | 823 | 407.14 | 4.07 |
| 2 | Backward Castes | 40 | 237 | 592.50 | 5.93 |
| 3 | Scheduled Cates | 51 | 377 | 739.21 | 7.39 |
| 4 | Scheduled Tribes | 07 | 53 | 757.14 | 7.57 |
| | **Total** | **300** | **1490** | **496.67** | **4.97** |

The data of the above table 4(13) shows that amongst 300 Muslims couples; an average fertility rate is found 4.97 i.e. 5 (approx.). But in general castes of

---

5Mathur Kank ; Socio-economic factors of Urban fertility : A case study of Shikohabad town of U.P., Published research paper, Magazine of Institute of Economic Growth, New Delhi, 2003, p. 13-19.

Muslims the average fertility rate is 4.07, in backward castes 5.93, in scheduled castes 7.39 and in scheduled tribes 7.57.

It is clear from the above table no. 4(14) that (i) the average effective age of marriage of the high status couples is 22.50 years, while achieved fertility period is 26.50 years, hence there is decrease of 7.50 yrs. in real fertility period, (ii) the average effective age of marriage of labour couples is 19.50 yrs., while achieved fertility period is 29.50 years, hence there is decrease of 4.50 years in real fertility period (iii) the average effective age of marriage due to dowry is 21 years, while achieved fertility period is 28 yrs.; hence there is decrease of 6 yrs. in real fertility period (iv) the average effective age of marriage among service holders & occupational couples is 25.50 years while achieved fertility period is 23.50 yrs.; hence there is decrease of 10.50 yrs. in real fertility period.

The researcher has also calculated the comparative fertility and fertility rates of females, who do use of contraceptives against child birth and those who do not. The following table no. 4(15) shows the comparison of fertility rates between these two types of surveyed females.............

From the analysis of the data of above table 4(15), it is clear that those women who use the contraceptives against births; the fertility rate is less than those women who do not use contraceptives against birth. It is noteworthy that amongst those women who use contraceptives against births, the average fertility rate is found 2.86, while those women who do not use contraceptives against births, the average fertility rate is found 4.17. Another conclusion is that "the fertility rate is inversely proportional to the fertile age groups" Therefore, it is suggested to increase the age of marriages; is the urgent need.

Separation & Divorce (Talaq):

It is not certain that after married, both the husband and wife will always have cordial relations.

There can be and usually are un-healthy and strained relations as well which result either in separation or Talaq. But Talaq and separation always does not mean low fertility. It is related to many factors i.e. how frequent is the separation, how much is the separation period, the age of the children, when the parents opt the separation or Talaq, age of the parents themselves at the time of separation or Talaq, the interval between the separation and re-marriage. Generally, it is seen that when length of separation and Talaq is more, the fertility will be less i.e. "The length of separation and Talaq is always inversely proportional to the fertility". But –

(1)    Those couples who have the tendency to live together have more fertility in comparison to those couples who live generally together.

(2)    Those couples who live together whenever have less fertility.

The researcher has also studied the fertility among those couples who used to live together and also among those who are separated and divorced. The following table no. 4(16) focuses on the fertility of the both above conditions.

**Table No. 4(16) : The presentation of fertility among the couples who used to live together; and also separated or divorced**

| S. No. | Couples | Frequencies of couples | Fertility per'000 women | Difference in fertility rate |
|--------|---------|------------------------|-------------------------|------------------------------|
| 1 | Those couples who used to live together | 263(87.67) | 371.90 | |
| 2 | Those couples who are separated or divorced (Talaq) | 37(12.33) | 197.00 | 170.90 |
| | Total | 300(100.00) | 359.26 | -- |

It is clear from the analysis of the data of above table no. 4(16) depicts, that the fertility rate of those couples who used to live together is found 371.90 per'000 women, while the fertility rate of those who are separated or divorce is found 197.0 per'000 women. Thus it may be conclude that the fertility rate decreases in the condition of separation and divorce/Talaq.

Prof. Kapadia (1960)[6] has stated that, the child marriages and widow re-marriages increase in fertility; therefore these traditions should be restricted, so that fertility rate may be reduced. Prof. Muthaiya[7] (2003) has also studied 13 cases of widows and concluded that, 'the fertility decreases by the period of widowhood'. He has stated the following four tables in evidence and clarification:

**Table No. 4(17) : 'Fertility and Widow re-marriage' : An evaluation**

| S. No. | Frequencies of Widows | % | Age group (in yrs.) at the time of widowhood | Age Groups (in yrs.) of re-marry | Period of Widowhood (in yrs.) | Decrease in fertile period (in yrs.) |
|---|---|---|---|---|---|---|
| 1 | 2 | 15.38 | below 16 | below 17 | 01.00 | 1.00 |
| 2 | 6 | 46.16 | 16 – 18 | | 2.50 | 2.50 |
| 3 | 3 | 23.08 | 18 – 22 | 17 – 22 | 4.50 | 4.50 |
| 4 | -- | 00.00 | 22 – 26 | 22 – 27 | -- | -- |
| 5 | 1 | 07.69 | 26 – 30 | 27 – 32 | 6.50 | 6.50 |
| 6 | -- | 00.00 | 30 – 34 | 32 – 37 | -- | -- |
| 7 | 1 | 07.69 | 34 – 38 | 37 – 42 | 8.50 | 8.50 |
| 8 | -- | 00.00 | more than 38 | 42 – 47 more than 47 | -- | -- |
| Total | 13 | 100.00 | | | -- | 1.77 i.e. 2 years. |

**Table No. 4(18) : Table showing the 'Number of Children' at the time of re-marriage**

| S.No. | No. of Children | Women who remarried | % |
|---|---|---|---|
| 1 | No. issues | 07 | 53.85 |
| 2 | 1 child | 04 | 30.77 |
| 3 | 2 children | 01 | 07.69 |
| 4 | 3 children | -- | 00.00 |
| 5 | 4 children | 01 | 07.69 |
| 6 | more than 4 | -- | 00.00 |
| | Total | 13 | 100.00 |

[6]Kapadia K.M. ; Family and Marriage in India, 1960, p. 210.

[7]Muthaiya M.N. ; Widowhood- A Demographic Survey in Six Villages of Mysore, Published research per in Magazine of Institute of Economic Growth, New Delhi, 2003, p. 48-54.

It is clear from the above table no. 4(18) that amongst 13 widows; 7(53.85%) become widows before the no issue, 4(30.77%) widows remarried having one child, 1(7.69%) widows having 2 children and only 1(7.69%) widow remarried having 4 children. The following table no. 4(19) shows the situation to which they did re-marriage:

**Table No. 4(19) : Situation of re-marriage to whom they married (Junior levirate, Senior levirate and others)**

| S. No. | Number of Children | To whom they married | | Total |
|---|---|---|---|---|
| | | With Junior & Senior levirates | Others | |
| 1 | No. issues | 3(23.08%) | 04(30.76%) | 07(53.85%) |
| 2 | 1 child | 2(15.38%) | 02(15.39%) | 04(30.77%) |
| 3 | 2 children | 1(07.39%) | --(00.00%) | 01(07.69%) |
| 4 | 3 children | --(00.00%) | --(00.00%) | --(00.00%) |
| 5 | 4 children | 1(07.69%) | --(00.00%) | 01(07.69%) |
| 6 | 5 children | --(00.00%) | --(00.00%) | --(00.00%) |
| | Total (%) | 7(53.85%) | 6(46.15%) | 13(100.00%) |

It was clear from the personal interviews that most of the cases of widow re-marriages are found in the illiterates, poor and lower sections of the Muslim communities. It is the noteworthy that the mother who has three or five children did not re-marry, but mostly sit down for their levirates or relatives. The researcher has asked the causes to do re-marry to all the 13 re-married female respondents. The following table no. 4(20) focuses on the reasons given by the female respondents:

**Table No. 4(20) : The reasons regarding re-marriage**

| S.No. | Causes responsible to re-marry | Frequencies | % |
|---|---|---|---|
| 1 | Without an issue (heirless) | 6 | 46.16 |
| 2 | To take care of children | 2 | 15.39 |
| 3 | To be success or of property | 4 | 30.76 |
| 4 | Being widow in early age | 1 | 07.69 |
| | Total | 13 | 100.00 |

The data of the above table shows that amongst 13 re-married Muslim women; 6(46.15%) remarry due to heirless, 2(15.39%) to take care of children, 4(30.76%) to be the successor of property and 1(7.69%) due to being widow in early age. The foregoing table shows the attitudes of the 300 couples i.e. of 600 respondents regarding issues:

## Table No. 4(21) : The attitudes of the couples towards issues (children)

| S. No. | Attitudes towards children/issues | Number of couples/respondents (%) | | Total (%) |
|---|---|---|---|---|
| | | Male | Females | |
| 1 | Less Issues | 119(19.83) | 141(23.50) | 260(43.33) |
| 2 | More Issues | 154(25.67) | 131(21.83) | 285(47.50) |
| 3 | Neutral response | 27(04.50) | 28(04.67) | 55(09.17) |
| | Total (%) | 300(50.00) | 300(50.00) | 600(100.00) |

*(Note: The figures shows in parenthesis are percentage)*

It is clear from the analysis of the data that amongst 300 Muslim couples, 260(43.33%) couples want less issues who are literate and service holders, 285(47.50%) more issues and 55(9.17%) couples have respond neutral regarding issues. In the light of above facts, it may conclude that majority of the Muslim couples want and have the desire of more issues. The following table no. 4(22) focuses on the opinions and the attitudes of 600 Muslim respondents towards the size of family:

## Table No. 4(22): The opinions & attitudes of the respondents towards the size of family

| S.No. | Attitudes in the favour of | Frequencies | % |
|---|---|---|---|
| 1 | Small size | 85 | 14.17 |
| 2 | Big size | 437 | 72.83 |
| 3 | Medium size | 78 | 13.00 |
| | Total | 600 | 100.00 |

The table no. 4(22) reveals that amongst 600 respondents of Muslim community; 85(14.17%) respondents are found in the fovour of small size of families, while only 78(13%) respondents medium size, but 437(72.83%) respondents have the desires of big size of the families; These respondents said that "the massage of our religion and angel (Prophet

Mohmmad$^{S.A.W}$) is: 'Do increase in Lineage; hence we are following. Secondly; our religion did not give the sanction of family planning. These are the two major reasons by which in our religion the families are found in big size.

At last, another question was asked to all 600 respondents, separately and individually at the time of personal interviews that according to your opinion, "what are those factors which can reduce fertility?" The responses given by the Muslim couple respondents are given in the following table no. 4(23):

**Table No. 4(23) : Responses to the question "what are those factors which can reduce fertility?" – according to the opinions of respondents**

| S. No. | The factors which can reduce fertility | The opinions of the respondents (frequencies & %) | | | | |
|---|---|---|---|---|---|---|
| | | in favour | in disfavour | Neutral | no response | Total |
| 1 | Late marriages | 380 (63.33) | 60 (10.00) | 148 (24.67) | 12 (02.00) | 600 (100.00) |
| 2 | Restrictions on early & child marriages | 450 (75.00) | 75 (12.50) | 75 (12.50) | -- (00.00) | 600 (100.00) |
| 3 | Separation & Divorces | 392 (65.33) | 98 (16.33) | 110 (18.34) | -- (00.00) | 600 (100.00) |
| 4 | Post partum Abistences (restrictions) | 376 (62.67) | 50 (08.33) | 168 (28.00) | 06 (01.00) | 600 (100.00) |
| 5 | Celibacy | 405 (67.50) | 72 (12.00) | 120 (10.00) | 03 (00.50) | 600 (100.00) |
| 6 | Tradition of dowry | 371 (61.83) | 60 (10.00) | 169 (28.17) | -- (00.00) | 600 (100.00) |
| 7 | Least frequencies of coitus | 443 (73.83) | 75 (12.50) | 82 (13.67) | -- (00.00) | 600 (100.00) |
| 8 | Use of contraceptives | 460 (76.67) | 40 (06.67) | 82 (13.66) | 18 (06.00) | 600 (100.00) |
| 9 | Mentality of small family | 395 (65.83) | 29 (04.83) | 170 (28.34) | 06 (01.00) | 600 (100.00) |
| 10 | Anti-attitudes of couples towards children | 403 (67.17) | 27 (04.50) | 150 (25.00) | 20 (03.33) | 600 (100.00) |
| 11 | More period of Talaq | 370 (61.67) | 100 (16.67) | 130 (21.66) | -- (00.00) | 600 (100.00) |
| 12 | Restrictions on re-marriages | 400 (66.67) | 67 (11.17) | 133 (22.16) | -- (00.00) | 600 (100.00) |
| 13 | Polygamy should be restricted | 445 (74.17) | 45 (07.50) | 95 (15.83) | 15 (02.50) | 600 (100.00) |
| 14 | Proper awareness among couples | 389 (64.83) | 75 (12.50) | 128 (21.33) | 08 (01.34) | 600 (100.00) |
| 15 | By enhancing family planning programmes | 405 (67.50) | 97 (16.17) | 92 (15.33) | 06 (01.00) | 600 (100.00) |

(Note: The figures shown in parentheses are percentage)

The table no. 4(23) depicts that amongst 600 Muslim respondents; regarding the factors which can reduce fertility, 380 (63.33%) have opined in the favour of late marriages, 450(75%) opined in the favour of restrictions on early and child marriages, 392(65.33%) opined in the favour of the post partum abistences, 405(67.50%) opined in the favour of the celibacy, 371(61.83%) opined in the favour of the tradition of dowry, 443(73.83%) opined in the favour of the least frequencies of coitus, 460(76.67%) opined in the favour of the use of contraceptives against births, 395(65.83%) opined in the favour of the mentality regarding small family, 403(67.17%) opined in the favour of the anti-attitudes of couples towards the births of the children, 370 (61.67%) opined in the favour of the Talaqs, 400(66.67%) opined in the favour of the restrictions on remarriages, 445(74.17%) opined in the favour of the polygamy should be restricted, 389(64.83%) opined in the favour to generate 'the proper awareness' among the couples and 405 (67.50%) respondents have opined that the fertility may be reduced 'by enhancing the family planning programmes' in Muslim families and communities.

In the light of the above discussion, it may be concluded that the factors as, late marriages, restrictions on early and child marriages, separation and divorces, restrictions on post partum- abistences, celibacy, tradition of dowry, least frequencies of coitus, use of contraceptives against births, mentality of small families among couples, anti-attitudes of couples towards children, more period of Talaq, restrictions on remarriages, restriction on the polygamy, proper awareness among the couples and by enhancing the family planning programmes in Muslim communities etc. factors may reduce; the rate of fertility may be reduced.

# Birth rate per'000 women & the fertility rate

Table No. 4(13)

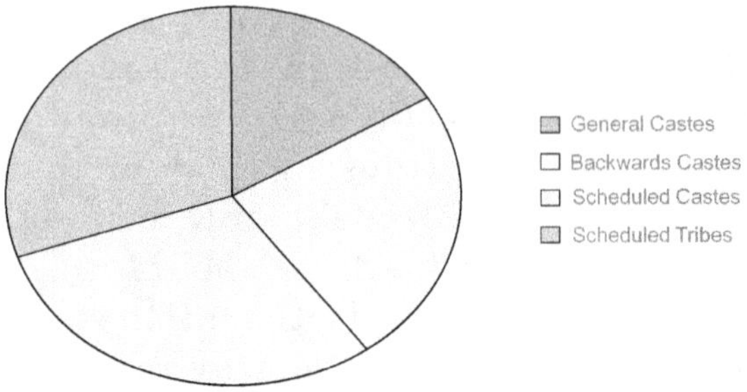

☐ General Castes
☐ Backwards Castes
☐ Scheduled Castes
☐ Scheduled Tribes

## The comparative study of surveyed females, who do use of contraceptives against child birth, and those who do not

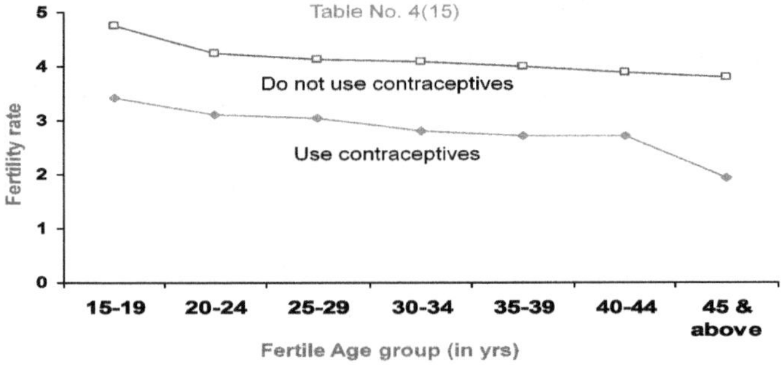

Table No. 4(15)

Do not use contraceptives

Use contraceptives

Fertility rate

Fertile Age group (in yrs)

15-19  20-24  25-29  30-34  35-39  40-44  45 & above

❖ ❖ ❖ ❖ ❖

# REFERENCES

1. Census of India (Report) 1931, Volume (1), Part-I.

2. Saxena R.K.; Social Factors of Fertility: A case study of slums of Kanpur city, A published paper in Quarterly Journal 'Samajik Sahyog' Ujjain (M.P.), 1989, p. 12.

3. National Sample Survey Organization (NSSO) Report 1964-65.

4. N.S.S.O. (Report): 2000-01, Office of the Registrar General of India, New Delhi, 2001.

5. Mathur Kank; Socio-economic factors of Urban fertility: A case study of Shikohabad Town of U.P.; Published research paper, Magazine of Institute of Economic Growth, New Delhi, 2003, p.13-19.

6. Kapadia K.M.; Family and Marriage in India, 1960, p. 210.

7. Muthaiya M.N.; Widowhood: A Demography Survey in Six villages of Mysore, Pub. Paper, Institute of Economic Growth, New Delhi, 2003, p.48-54.

# CHAPTER 5
# Economic Factors and Fertility

The fertility rate in urban areas is almost everywhere lower than that of the rural areas. The influence of economic status however, working in favour of lower fertility, crosses this tendency to show that even in rural areas fertility is lower in higher economic level groups as compared to fertility in urban areas in lower economic groups. However, other studies have not shown so much specific influence of economic status upon fertility. **Driver's** study has shown fertility rate of 4.5 for all income groups while it was 4.6 both for monthly income below 500 and above 2000.[*] It may be noted that similar results were obtained by **Prof. Mukerjee** and **Baljit** when they showed that the fertility rate in Rs. 500-1000 monthly income groups was 3.3 uniformly.[**]

Studies by several sociologists have shown that occupation is a fertility differential in India. In some cases however, this has not been clearly confirmed. For example, according to Mysore Study the average number of children born alive to couples in high professional and managerial workers as well as among domestic and other services workers was uniformly 5.0. However, other studies have shown some distinction. For example, **G.B. Saxena** in his study of differential fertility in rural Uttar Pradesh, shows that while the fertility for service class was 6.4 and business and artisans 6.6, the fertility among agriculturists was 7.1 and among labourers as much as 7.8. The general tendency of higher fertility among occupations of cultivation and manual labour has been confirmed by so many other studies in India. The fertility rate of clerical workers was found to be lowest in his study by E.D. Driver.[*]All

---

[*]Driver, E.D., Differential Fertility in Central India, p. 88.
[**]Mukerjee, R.K., and Baljit Singh, Social Profiles of a Metropolis, p. 167.
[*]Driver, E.D., Differential Fertility in Central India, p. 93.

these studies show that there is some influence of occupation upon fertility among cultivators and labourers. Equal importance must be given to illiteracy and lower economic and educational status.

Among the theories of fertility; laying emphasis upon economic factors of fertility, the following two theories have been important contributions to the economic interpretation of fertility:

**(1) Liebensteins Theory**[1]**:** In his book, 'Economic Backwardness and Economic Growth' (1957), Harvey Liebenstein formulated a theory which explained the factors determining the number of children desired by each couple. It was based upon the assumption that people calculate the number of children they should have on the basis of satisfactions or utilities and cost both monitory and psychological. The types of utilities derived are: (a) The utility of the child as consumption good or a source of pleasure (b) The utility as a productive unit and (c) The utility as a source of security in the old age. The two types of costs involved are direct costs and indirect costs. The former include conventional current expenses and the latter include opportunities foregone due to the additional child. According to Liebenstein the following three chances occur due to the effect of utilities and costs: income effect, survival effect and occupational distribution effect. Demographer **(Prof.) Harvey Liebenstein** pointed out that this framework can be used, "To draw the relationship in such a way that, in general, the outcome is such that as the per capita income grows, the number of high parity children for the representative family falls." This theory has been accepted to be explanatory rather than predictive.

**(b) Backer's Theory**[2]**:** Backer (1960) presented his economic theory of fertility in his article entitled, 'An Economic Analysis of fertility'. He applied micro-consumption theory to fertility and argued that fertility behaviour is the result of household choice. The choice of purchase of durable goods is made after a careful evaluation of the utilities derived and the costs incurred. Treating children as household commodities, **Prof. Backer** argued that a couple's decision in this respect depends on the balance of preferences, the constraints of income and the costs of the child. If the knowledge of

---

[1]Harvey Liebenstein ; "An interpretation of the Economic Theory of Fertility" Journal of Economic Literature, Vol. 12, 1974, p. 460.

[2]Sharma R.N. (et.al.); Demography and population problems, Raj Hans Pub., Meerut, 2001, p. 171.

birth control were widespread, fertility would be directly related to the income. This theory has been criticized by **Liebenstein** and **Judith Black**. Baker's attitude regarding the fertility is based on economic behaviour of the household.

In Demographic Year Book[3] (1988), office of the Registrar General of India, New Delhi, has stated, 'the socio-economic factors of fertility'; these include : educational attainment, economic status, occupation of the husband, employment of wife, economic groups, industrialization, food supply, economic conditions, desire to maintain status, poverty and economic majesty etc..

According to **Prof. Sharma Rajendra K.**[4] **(2005),** there becomes an inverse relationship between educational attainment particularly of the woman and the fertility rate. The higher the educational level, the lower is the family size. However, at the highest educational level the curve has shown an upward tendency of direction. Educational attainment shows a negative co-relationship with fertility. It is because the educated women marry at a higher age. They also use more sophisticated methods of birth control and also more often.

As investigator **(Mrs.) Agrawala**[5] **(2007)** has found in her empirical study of "Socio-economic determinants of fertility", that economic status has an inverse relationship with fertility.

Demographer **Agrawal S.N.**[6] **(1970)** has observed in his studies that, 'fertility rate goes down with higher economic statuses'. Inverse relationship between economic status and fertility has been also observed in India in three rounds of the National Sample Survey in 1959-60, 1960-61 and 1961-62.

According to **S.N. Agrawala**[7] **(1970:103),** "The cultivators has an average 7.4 children while those in services and professions has an average of 6.6 children".

According to **Edwin D. Driver**[8] **(1963:93),** "The wives of un-skilled workers, agriculturists and artisans have higher fertility as compared to the wives of the clerks".

**(Mrs.) Malhotra Suneeta**[9] **(2009)** presented a paper entitled, "Employed women and fertility" A study based on 50 educated employed mothers of Gwalior city of M.P. She concluded on the basis of her field study that employed mothers have a negative relationship with fertility, though its' exact nature has not been established. One does not know whether women having smaller children go out for jobs or those who have jobs produce few children. Perhaps both the reasons may be equally important. It is noticed that most of the educated ladies without children take up jobs. On the other hand, most of the women on jobs, practice methods of birth control and restrict their families according to their desires.

In general 'Economic Factors' include industrialization and higher standard of living has compelled so many males to stay in urban areas away from their females resulting in lower birth rate. Raising of the standard of living has led to the desire for a small family to maintain the standard. Therefore, in the higher economic groups in developed societies, the birth rate is fallen very appreciably, so much so that childlessness is an increasing phenomenon. In the view of investigator social factors today are closely linked with economic factors. In fact social factors are the most important determinants of the present fertility rate. The most important social and economic factors determining fertility are as follows : **(i) Urban Society;** as compared to the rural society, lays more emphasis upon enjoyment, individualism, small family, high standard of living, social change etc. Almost all the characteristics of modern society favour low fertility. **(ii) Modern Family;** with all its characteristics, has led to lower birth rate. The ideal of high standard of living, more education for children, more health care of the female and the children etc. have motivated to two children and even to one. For the same reason the tendency of not marrying, marry at late age, marrying temporarily and sex enjoyment as the main purpose of marriage have resulted low fertility **(iii) Higher Standard of living;** high standard of living and the high cost of the budgets have considerably inflated family budgets. Therefore, efforts have to be made to keep the family strictly limited to meet the high costs of living and bring up children **(iv) Economic Factors;** widespread poverty leads to illiteracy, lower standard of living and corresponding high fertility. The children in lower economic group very soon start helps their parents in earning their living. Therefore the number of children is rather a welcome factor. Again, 'lower economic status' leads to **fatalism**[*] motivate high fertility.

---

[*] Fatalism in India, is significant motivating factor, has been the fatalistic attitude such as the 'Theory of Karma'; according to which, "Children are the gift of God". Similar views have been expressed by Muslim respondents 'Allah' is all in all (he)

On the basis of his empirical study **Qureshi**[10] **(2009)** draw some conclusions as under: (i) the fertility becomes low in higher income groups in comparison to medium and low income groups. (ii) The rate of fertility becomes low in service holders and businessmen in comparison to agriculturists and labours. (iii) The fertility becomes more in housewives in comparison to occupationists and serving wives. (iv) The shortage of food supply becomes directly proportional to fertility and (v) the economic conditions of families become directly linked with fertility.

Undoubtedly, it is true that the economic factors affect birth rate and fertility directly or indirectly; in which economic status of family, occupations, food supply and economic pressure, expenditure of family, conditions of employment, chances of employment, source of income, participation of women in the income of family, economic majesty etc. are important and notable factors, which play significant roles. In his study **Prof. Pant**[11] **(1990:230)** has taken, income groups, occupational structure, standard of living, food supply etc. economic factors as determinants of fertility, but **Prof. Hans Raj**[12] **(1978:74-75)** has explained economic conditions, standard of living, chances of employment for growing population, children a source of income or burden on the parents, expenses of family, economic sources of family, women's participation in economy, employed woman, employed couples etc. as affecting factors of birth rate and fertility. First of all, the researcher has studied the effect of income-groups on the birth rate of children. The following table no. 5(1) focuses on the income-groups and birth rate of children per'000 women and on average issues/children per surveyed Muslim women:

said the same; therefore the fatalism is a responsible factor for motivating high fertility.

## Table No. 5(1) : Lower Income-group & no. of issues per'000 women

| S. No. | Monthly income (in Rs.) | Frequencies of couples | Total no. of alive children | Children per couple | Number of children per'000 women (Fertility) |
|---|---|---|---|---|---|
| 1 | below 500 | 06 | 46 | 7.667 | 7667 |
| 2 | 500 – 1000 | 36 | 217 | 6.027 | 6027 |
| 3 | 1000 – 1500 | 40 | 233 | 5.825 | 5825 |
| 4 | 1500 – 2000 | 58 | 301 | 5.189 | 5189 |
| 5 | 2000 – 2500 | 72 | 346 | 4.805 | 4805 |
| | Total | 212 | 1143 | 5.391 | 5391 |

The data of above table shows that amongst the 212 couples of lower income groups; the fertility of the couples of income group below Rs. 500 is 7667, the fertility of the couples of income group Rs. 500-1000 is 6027, the fertility of the couples of income group Rs. 1000-1500 is 5825, the fertility of the couples of income group Rs. 1500-2000 is 5189, and the fertility of the couples of income group Rs. 2000-2500 is found 4805. In the light of above facts, it may be concluded that "the fertility is inversely proportional to the income groups".

The following table 5(2) shows the number of children per'000 women (fertility) among the couples of medium income groups.

## Table No. 5(2) : The fertility among the couples of medium income groups

| S. No. | Monthly income (in Rs.) | Frequencies of couples | Total no. of alive children | Children per couple | Number of children per'000 women (Fertility) |
|---|---|---|---|---|---|
| 1 | 2500 – 3000 | 24 | 69 | 2.875 | 2875 |
| 2 | 3000 – 3500 | 20 | 51 | 2.550 | 2551 |
| 3 | 3500 – 4000 | 18 | 36 | 2.0 | 2000 |
| | Total | 62 | 156 | 2.52 | 2526 |

The data of above table 5(2) shows that amongst 62 couples of medium income groups; the fertility of the couples of income group Rs. 2500-3000 is found 2875, the fertility of the couples of income group Rs. 3000-3500 is found 2551 and the fertility of income group Rs. 3500 to 4000 is found 2000 per'000 women. The following table no. 5(3) shows the number of children per'000 women/fertility among the couples of high income-groups:

## Table No. 5(3) : The fertility among the couples of high income groups

| S. No. | Monthly Income (in Rs.) | Frequencies of couples | Total no. of alive children | Children per couple | Number of children per'000 women (Fertility) |
|---|---|---|---|---|---|
| 1 | 4000 – 4500 | 12 | 20 | 1.67 | 1666 |
| 2 | 4500 – 5000 | 09 | 14 | 1.56 | 1556 |
| 3 | above than 5000 | 10 | 19 | 1.90 | 1900 |
| | Total | 26 | 53 | 2.04 | 2038 |

The data of above table no. 5(3) focuses that amongst 26 couples of Muslims of high income groups; the fertility of the couples of income group Rs. 4000-4500 is found 1666, the fertility of the couples of the income group Rs. 4500-5000 is found 1556, and the fertility of income- groups Rs. above than 5000 is found 1900 per'000 women.

In the light of the data of the tables no. 5(1), 5(2) and 5(3); it is clear that: (1) "The fertility becomes inversely proportional to the income-groups". (2) "The birth rate of children in lower income-groups becomes high in comparison to the higher income groups".

The researcher has also tried to know the relationship between expenditure and fertility, and he calculate the fertility or births of children per'000 women on the basis of the expenditure of their families. The following table 5(4) focuses on the number of children per couple and fertility per'000 women on the basis of monthly expenditure:

Table No. 5(4): Monthly expenditure (in Rs.) and fertility per'000 women

| S. No. | Monthly expenditure group (in Rs.) | Number of couples | No. of alive children | No. of Children per couple | Fertility per'000 women |
|---|---|---|---|---|---|
| 1 | 500 – 1000 | 10 | 67 | 6.7 | 6700 |
| 2 | 1000 – 1500 | 17 | 103 | 6.05 | 6058 |
| 3 | 1500 – 2000 | 20 | 104 | 5.20 | 5200 |
| 4 | 2000 – 2500 | 75 | 372 | 4.96 | 4960 |
| 5 | 2500 – 3000 | 98 | 486 | 4.95 | 4959 |
| 6 | 3000 – 3500 | 40 | 127 | 3.17 | 3175 |
| 7 | 3500 – 4000 | 38 | 89 | 2.34 | 2342 |
| 8 | above than 4000 | 02 | 04 | 2.00 | 2000 |
| | Total | 300 | 1352 | 4.50 | 4500 |

The data of above table 5(4) focuses that amongst 300 Muslim couples; the fertility of expenditure group Rs. 500-1000 is found 6700, the fertility of expenditure group Rs. 1000-1500 is found

6058, the fertility of expenditure group Rs. 1500-2000 is found 5200,the fertility of expenditure group Rs. 2000-2500 is found 4960, the fertility of expenditure group Rs. 2500-3000 is found 4959, the fertility of expenditure group Rs. 3000-3500 is found 3175, the fertility of expenditure group Rs. 3500-4000 is found 2342 and fertility 2000 per'000 women is found (which is least) in the expenditure group above than 4000 Rs. In the light of the above figures and facts, it may conclude that "there is an inverse relationship between the expenditure groups and fertility."

**Prof. Malthus** clarifies in his theory, that in societies where "there is shortage of food supply, there is less fertility". But many demographers have found through their empirical studies that being the problem of the food supply among the families of labours and artisans, the number of children become more. Hence, the statement of **Prof. Malthus** is not seen true and significant. Here it is noteworthy that the statistical calculation of the food supply per day/family/individual is not so easy; therefore the observatory conclusion is giving here. At the time of interview the respondents replied that, "the children become the stick of old age". Again, the researcher has asked that, "Have you ever killed your baby/child in the shortage of the food supply?" Then, cent-percent respondents responded in negative. It is well known fact, that 'coitus' is the **biological need and necessity of human being; so, it (coitus) is not co-related with the supply of food in any sense. Therefore, it is impossible to** co-relate between 'the fertility and food supply' from the sociological view-point.

Generally, the economists say that, 'the economic pressure and fertility' becomes directly co-related and are reciprocal to each other.* The foregoing table nos. 5(5), 5(6) and 5(7) focus in brief, on the type of family and fertility, occupations and fertility and the nature of employment and fertility. The following table no. 5(5) shows the relationship between the type of family and fertility:

---

*Bertrand Russell (neo-economist), 'Theory of Population' quoted from Thompson E. and Levis; Population Problems, Mc-Graw Hill Book Co., 1978, p. 110.

Table No. 5(5) : Type of families and fertility per family [See table no. 3(3)]

| S. No. | Type of family | Total no. of families | No. of alive births in total fertile period | Fertility per family | Approximate fertility rate |
|--------|----------------|-----------------------|---------------------------------------------|----------------------|----------------------------|
| 1 | Joint family | 163 | 789 | 4.84 | 4.8 |
| 2 | Nuclear family | 120 | 506 | 4.21 | 4.2 |
| 3 | Extended family | 17 | 57 | 3.35 | 3.4 |
| | **Total** | **300** | **1352** | **4.50** | **4.50** |

It is clear from the analysis of the data of above table no. 5(5) that amongst 300 surveyed families; the fertility rate per family is found (approximately) 4.8 among 163 joint families, 4.2 among 120 nuclear families and 3.4 among the 17 extended families; while on an average fertility rate per family is found 4.50. It is noteworthy (in the light of above facts) that 'the rate of fertility is found more in Joint families, in comparison to the nuclear and extended families'. The following table no. 5(6) shows the occupational structure and fertility level among the surveyed 300 Muslim families:

Table No. 5(6) : The occupations of families and fertility per family [See table no. 3(9)]

| S. No. | Occupations of families | Total no. of families (couples) | No. of alive births in total fertile period | Fertility per couple | Approximate fertility rate |
|--------|-------------------------|---------------------------------|---------------------------------------------|----------------------|----------------------------|
| 1 | Agriculture | 200 | 871 | 4.36 | 4.4 |
| 2 | Labour | 50 | 327 | 6.29 | 6.3 |
| 3 | Shop keeping | 09 | 49 | 5.44 | 5.4 |
| 4 | Service | 18 | 56 | 3.11 | 3.1 |
| 5 | Other | 21 | 49 | 2.33 | 2.3 |
| | Total | 300 | 1352 | 4.50 | 4.50 |

The analysis of the figures of the above table no. 5(6) shows that:

(1)     The maximum fertility is found in the labours.

(2)     The minimum fertility is found in the service holders and others i.e. who are doing better services.

It is clear that in the surveyed 300 families, the average fertility rate is found 4.50 (approx.), among the families of agriculturists the fertility rate is 4.4, among the labour's families the fertility rate is 6.3 (maximum), among shopkeepers/businessmen families the fertility rate is 5.4, among the families of service holders, fertility rate is found 3.1 (minimum) and other families, who's couples are doing better services, it is 2.3 (lowest).

It is the law of science physics that "the mobility and weight becomes in inversely proportion". It seems true in demography also. It is seen, at the time of survey that, 'the more children become the source of income in the views of the labours and the families of lower income groups' while children; a responsibility in the families of higher income groups. Hence, the poor's want and have the desires of more issues. In this way the poor families produce more children in comparison to the rich families. The following table no. 5(7) focuses on the comparative fertility of the couples of daily wage and permanent job holders:

### Table No. 5(7) : Nature of Jobs & Fertility/no. of children per couple

| S. No. | Nature of Jobs | Total no. of families (couples) | No. of alive births in total fertile period | No. of children per couple (fertility) | |
|---|---|---|---|---|---|
| | | | | Complete value | approximate value |
| 1 | Daily wage | 52 | 327 | 6.29 | 6.3 |
| 2 | Permanent | 18 | 56 | 3.11 | 3.1 |
| | Total | 70 | 383 | 5.47 | 5.5 |

The table no. 5(7) depicts that the fertility of daily wage couples (6.3) is more than the fertility (3.1) of the couples who are doing permanent jobs. The number of the children is found in the ratio of 2:1 in the surveyed daily wage and permanent job's families respectively.

According to the demographer **Prof. Hans Raj;** the occupational structure plays the significant and important role in fertility. The foregoing tables focus on the corresponding matter:

## Table No. 5(8): Occupations of husband's and fertility rates

| S. No. | Occupations of husbands of female respondents | Frequencies of wives | No. of alive births (in ten years) | Average no. of children per woman | Fertility Rate (approx.) |
|---|---|---|---|---|---|
| 1 | Agriculture | 200 | 871 | 4.39 | 4.4 |
| 2 | Labour (Physical) | 52 | 352 | 6.77 | 6.8 |
| 3 | Job/Service | 18 | 56 | 3.82 | 3.8 |
| 4 | Shopkeeping/Business | 09 | 49 | 5.44 | 5.4 |
| 5 | Other | 21 | 49 | 2.33 | 2.3 |
| | Total | 300 | 1352 | 4.55 | 4.6 |

The figures of the above table no. 5(8) shows that amongst 300 surveyed families; the fertility rate among the agriculturists families is 4.4, while in those families who do physical labour is 6.8 (maximum); the fertility rate in job holders' families is 3.8, in Shopkeepers and businessmen is 5.4 and 2.3 (minimum) in others; those who do higher jobs/services. The following table no. 5(9) focuses on the annual income of wives and their respective fertility rates:

## Table No. 5(9) : The annual income of wives & fertility rates

| S. No. | Annual income of wives (in Rs.) | No. of wives | No. of alive births in total fertile period | Fertility per woman | Fertility Rate |
|---|---|---|---|---|---|
| 1 | less than 2000 | 24 | 135 | 6.43 | 6.4 |
| 2 | 2000 – 4000 | 75 | 418 | 5.57 | 5.6 |
| 3 | 4000 – 6000 | 50 | 231 | 4.62 | 4.6 |
| 4 | 6000 – 8000 | 39 | 163 | 4.18 | 4.2 |
| 5 | 8000 – 10000 | 62 | 249 | 4.02 | 4.0 |
| 6 | more than 10000 | 50 | 156 | 3.12 | 3.1 |
| | Total | 300 | 1352 | 4.55 | 4.6 |

The analysis of the data of above table no. 5(9) shows that those wives whose annual income is more than 10000 Rs., the fertility rate is 3.1 (lowest); while the fertility rate is found 6.4 (highest) among those wives whose annual income is less than Rs. 2000. In the light of these facts and figures; it may conclude that, "Income and fertility becomes inversely proportional to each other".

It is notable here, that amongst 300 surveyed Muslim couples; 259 wives are pure housewives, 24 daily wage labours, 4 temporary teachers of basic and 13 wives are others; whose source of livelihood are rope making, tailoring, rosemary and plate making by leaves etc. The following table no. 5(10) shows the occupations of wives and their corresponding fertilities:

**Table No. 5(10) : The Occupations of wives, No. of children per woman & their corresponding fertilities**

| S. No. | Occupations of wife respondents | Frequencies & wives | Total number of births/ children | Number of children per women | Fertility Rate (approximate) |
|---|---|---|---|---|---|
| 1 | Pure housewives | 259 | 1209 | 4.67 | 4.7 |
| 2 | Temporary basic Teacher | 04 | 10 | 2.50 | 2.5 |
| 3 | Daily Wage labours | 24 | 121 | 5.41 | 5.4 |
| 4 | Others: (Rope making, Tailoring, rosemary & plate making by leaves, etc.) | 13 | 52 | 4.00 | 4.0 |
| | **Total** | **300** | **1352** | **4.55** | **4.6** |

It is clear from the analysis of the data of above table no. 5(10) that amongst 300 wives; the fertility rate of pure housewives is 4.7; while the fertility rate among the wives of daily wage labours is found 5.4 (highest); the fertility rate of other's wives, whose occupations are rope making, tailoring and rosemary and plate making by leaves etc., is found 4.0, but the fertility rate among temporary basic teacher is 2.5, which is lowest. It is clear from the above discussion that the rate of fertility is found less among the self depend women, in comparison to others. In other words, it may state that employed women are found in the favour of limited families, while the house-wives in big families. The following table no. 5(11) shows the distribution of female respondents with respect to the structure of their occupations:

**Table No. 5(11) : Distribution of female respondents with respect to their occupational structure**

| S. No. | Occupations | Number of female respondents according to their occupations | | | | |
|---|---|---|---|---|---|---|
| | | House wives | Temporary teachers | Daily wage | Others | Total |
| 1 | Main | 259 | 01 | -- | 01 | 261 |
| 2 | Subsidiary | -- | 03 | 24 | 12 | 39 |
| | **Total** | **259** | **04** | **24** | **13** | **300** |

The table no. 5(11) shows that amongst 300 Muslim woman respondents, 261 respondents are engaged in various main occupations and 39 respondents in different subsidiary occupations. It is clear, that those wives who are engaged in subsidiary occupations with main occupations; are co-operating in economic activities of their families. The following table no. 5(12) shows the fertility among the women on the basis of main and subsidiary occupations:

**Table No. 5(12) : The presentation of fertility among the women respondents on the basis of main & subsidiary occupations**

| S. No. | Occupations of the women respondents | Women of main occupations | | | Women of subsidiary occupations | | |
|---|---|---|---|---|---|---|---|
| | | Frequencies | Total no. of issues | Fertility Rate | Frequencies | Total no. of issues | Fertility Rate |
| 1 | Housewives | 259 | 1209 | 4.7 | -- | -- | -- |
| 2 | Temporary Teacher | 01 | 03 | 3.0 | 03 | 07 | 2.3 |
| 3 | Daily wage Labour | -- | -- | -- | 24 | 121 | 5.04 |
| 4 | Others (Rope making, Tailoring, rosemary and plate making by leaves etc.) | 01 | 05 | 5.0 | 12 | 47 | 3.9 |
| | Grand Total | 261 | 1217 | 4.66 | 39 | 175 | 4.5 |

It is clear from the analysis of the data of the above table no. 5(12) that the fertility rate among the women who are engaged in main occupations is 4.66 (higher), than those women, who are engaged in different subsidiary occupations.

The following table no. 5(13) shows the attitudes of the 39 working women towards the births of children and the size of family:

**Table No. 5(13) : The attitudes of the working women towards the births of children and the size of family**

| S.No. | The attitudes of the working women towards the births of children & size of family | Frequencies of employed women | Percentage |
|---|---|---|---|
| 1 | No issues/child less | -- | 00.00 |
| 2 | 1 child | 10 | 25.64 |
| 3 | 2 children | 26 | 66.67 |
| 4 | 3 children | 03 | 07.69 |
| 5 | 4 children | -- | 00.00 |
| 6 | more than 4 children | -- | 00.00 |
| | Total | 39 | 100.00 |

It is clear from the data of above table no. 5(13) that: (1) The children become the basic necessity of the family, therefore no woman have accepted self without issue/child; 10(25.64%) working women have the desire of the family of one issue, 26(66.67%) working women have the desire of the family of 2 children; while only 3(7.69%) working women have the desire of the family of 3 children. In the light of the above facts, it may conclude that 90% working women want one or two issues only and believe in the limited family for the sake of the employment and to do job. I asked further to all the 39 working women that "why do you want limited family and less issues?" The following table 5(14) shows the responses given by the 39 women respondents:

**Table No. 5(14) : "Why do you want limited family & less issues?"**
**-Responses to the question**

| S. No. | Responses to the question (given by 39 working women) | Frequencies | % |
|--------|-------------------------------------------------------|-------------|-----|
| 1 | More children, more burden | 09 | 23.08 |
| 2 | To save herself from family responsibilities and liabilities | 06 | 15.38 |
| 3 | More children hinder in work/job | 10 | 25.64 |
| 4 | For personal/individual freedom | 09 | 23.08 |
| 5 | To go through proper care, better education & career (future) of children | 05 | 12.82 |
| | Total | 39 | 100.00 |

Amongst 39 working women respondents; 9(23.08%) respondents have answered that they want limited family and less issues because 'more children become more burden', 6(15.38%) respondents respond 'to save herself from the family responsibilities' and burden, 10(25.64%) respondents said 'more children hinder in work', 9(23.08%) respond 'for personal freedom' and only 5(12.82%) respondents have answered 'to go through proper care, better education and career of the children'. But in the view of the investigator the most of the respondents have told more than one reason. Which are shown in the foregoing table 5(15):

**Table No. 5(15) : Presentation of the responses to the question "why do you want limited family & less issues?"**

| S.No. | Single and multiple responses | Frequencies (%) |
|---|---|---|
| 1 | To save herself from family responsibilities | 06(15.38%) |
| 2 | More children hinder in work/job | 10(25.64%) |
| 3 | For individual freedom | 23(58.97%) |
| 4 | (a + b) | 16(41.03%) |
| 5 | (b + c) | 33(84.62%) |
| 6 | (c + a) | 29(74.36%) |
| 7 | (a + b + c) | 39(100.00%) |

(Note: The total number of percentage is more than 100% due to multiple responses)

*Symbols:*    a = to save herself from family responsibilities/liabilities
             b = more children hinder in work
             c = for individual (personal) freedom

Here, it is noteworthy that most of the respondents told that the reasons for the 'limited (small) family and less issues' are to save herself from the family liabilities and responsibilities, more issues hinder in work and for the sake of individual freedom.

The following table no. 5(16) shows the attitudes of all 39 working women respondents; regarding the causes; to have her family limited and fewer issues.

**Table No. 5(16) : The attitudes of women respondents regarding the causes to have the family limited & less issues : According to Likert' attitude scale [as per table no. 5(14)]**

| S. No. | Various causes responsible for limited family & less issues | Attitudes of the respondents (frequencies/%) | | | | | Total (%) |
|---|---|---|---|---|---|---|---|
| | | Totally agree | Agree | Neutral | Disagree | Totally disagree | |
| 1 | More children, more burden | 13 (33.33) | 12 (30.76) | 08 (20.51) | 02 (05.13) | 04 (10.26) | 39 (100.00) |
| 2 | To save herself from family responsibilities & liabilities | 16 (41.02) | 09 (23.08) | 04 (10.26) | 04 (10.26) | 06 (15.38) | 39 (100.00) |
| 3 | More issues hinder in work/job | 25 (64.11) | 06 (15.38) | -- (00.00) | 06 (15.38) | 02 (05.13) | 39 (100.00) |
| 4 | For personal/individual freedom | 15 (38.46) | 13 (33.33) | 07 (17.95) | 03 (07.69) | 01 (02.50) | 39 (100.00) |
| 5 | To proper care, better education & career (future) of issues | 27 (69.23) | 08 (20.51) | 02 (05.13) | 02 (05.13) | -- (00.00) | 39 (100.00) |

(Note: The figures given in parenthesis are percentage of frequencies)

From the above table no. 5(16), it is clear that amongst 39 working women respondents:

(1)    13(33.33%) respondents are found totally agree in the favour of limited family and less issues, 12(30.76%) agree, 8(20.51%) neutral, 2(5.13%) disagree and 4(10.26%) totally disagree with the reason 'more children, more burden'.

(2)    16(41.02%) respondents are found totally agree in the favour of limited family and less issues, 9(23.08%) agree, 4(10.26%) neutral, 4(10.26%) disagree and 6(15.8%) totally disagree with the reason 'to save herself from the family responsibilities and liabilities'.

(3)    25(64.11%) respondents are found totally agree in favour of limited family and less issues, 6(15.38%) agree, 6(15.38%) totally disagree and 2(5.13%) respondents disagree with the reason 'more issues hinder in work'.

(4)    15(38.46%) respondents are found totally agree in the favour of limited family and less issues, 13(33.33%) agree, 7(17.95%) neutral, 3(7.69%) disagree and only 1(2.50%) totally disagree with the reason 'for personal freedom'.

(5)    27(69.23%) respondents are found totally agree in the favour of limited family and less issues, 8(20.51%) agree, 2(5.13%) neutral and 2(5.13%) respondents disagree with the reasons i.e. 'to **proper care, better education and for better future/career of children'.**

In the light of the data and figures of S.No.(5), it is concluded that 35(89.74%) women respondents want limited family and less issues due to; to do proper care of them, to give better education and for the betterment of career of the children/issues.

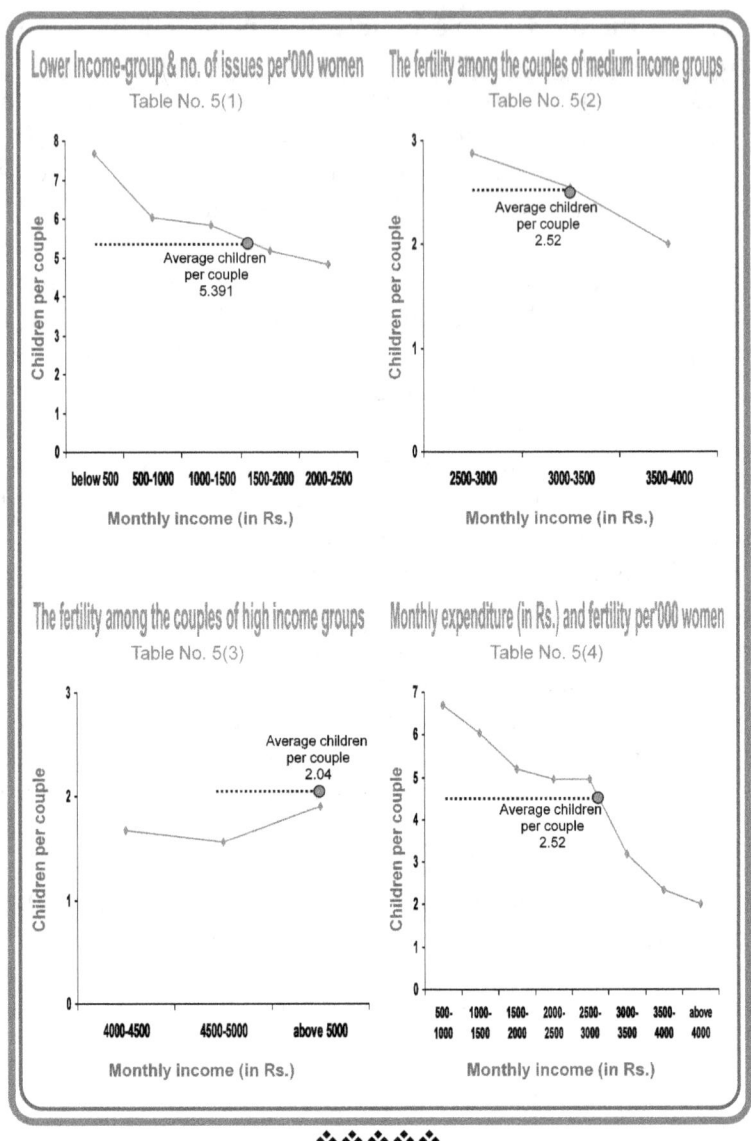

**Lower Income-group & no. of issues per'000 women**
Table No. 5(1)

Children per couple (y-axis)
Monthly income (in Rs.)
below 500, 500-1000, 1000-1500, 1500-2000, 2000-2500

Average children
per couple
5.391

**The fertility among the couples of medium income groups**
Table No. 5(2)

Children per couple
Monthly income (in Rs.)
2500-3000, 3000-3500, 3500-4000

Average children
per couple
2.52

**The fertility among the couples of high income groups**
Table No. 5(3)

Children per couple
Monthly income (in Rs.)
4000-4500, 4500-5000, above 5000

Average children
per couple
2.04

**Monthly expenditure (in Rs.) and fertility per'000 women**
Table No. 5(4)

Children per couple
Monthly income (in Rs.)
500-1000, 1000-1500, 1500-2000, 2000-2500, 2500-3000, 3000-3500, 3500-4000, above 4000

Average children
per couple
2.52

❖ ❖ ❖ ❖ ❖

# REFERENCES

1.  Harvey Liebenstein; An Interpretation of the 'Economic Theory of Fertility' Journal of Economic Literature, Vol. 12, 1974, p. 460.

2.  Sharma Ram Nath; Demography and Population Problems, Raj Hans Publications, Ram Nagar, Meerut, 2001, p. 171.

3.  Demographic year Book; Office of the Registrar General of India, New Delhi, 1998, p. 69.

4.  Sharma Rajendra K.; 'Education and Fertility': A study based on 200 married educated women of Ghaziabad city; Published Article, Journal of Family Welfare, Vol. 23, No. 11, June 2005, p. 25-30.

5.  Agrawala Kavita ; An Empirical Study of 'Socio-Economic Determinants of Fertility', Published Article, Journal of Demography, I.I.F.P., Bombay (Andheri), Vol. 6, No. 4, Dec. 2007.

6.  Agrawal S.N. ; A Demographic Survey of Six Urbanizing Villages, Asia Publishing House, Bombay, 1970, p. 102-103.

7.  Agrawal S.N. ; A Demographic Survey of Six Urbanizing Villages, Asia Publishing House, Bombay, 1970, p. 102-103.

8.  Driver Edwin D.; Fertility in Central India, Princeton Univ. Press, Princeton, 1963, p. 93.

9.  Malhotra Suneeta ; ' Employed Women and Fertility' Published paper, Seminar Ank, M.L.B. (Autonomous) College Gwalior (M.P.), Seminar Conducted on 23 & 24 Feb. 2009, p. 20-27.

10. Quresi, Azamal; 'Economic Determinants and Fertility': An analysis, paper submitted in Seminar, Organized by M.L.B. (Autonomous) college Gwalior, on 23 & 24 Feb. 2009.

11. **Pant J.C.; Demography, Goel Publishing House, Meerut, 1990, p.230.**

12. Hans Raj; Fundamentals of Demography: Population Studies with Special reference to India, Surjeet Pub. House, Delhi, 1978, p. 74-75.

# CHAPTER 6
# Educational Status and Fertility Level

'Education' is one of the most important social determinants of fertility because it serves the 'motivation' aspect of family limitation. Education should be of a greater importance as a determining factor with regard to reduction. Action can be taken on this front easily and in the most effective manner. We can achieve better results as far as educating the people is concerned. We can't urbanize, industrialize, raise the standard of living, break the joint family system, change the occupational structure and effectively raise the marriage age in a conceivable short period of time as easily as we can educate our people.

Several studies have pointed out an inverse co-relation between education and fertility. The Mysore study pointed out that in Bangalore city the average number of children born to females of the age of 50 and who were illiterate was between 5.3 and 5.5. No significant difference was found in the fertility of illiterates and moment educated up to middle school standard. However, the fertility rate of woman educated up to High School or more was only 3.9. This is not only due to a better knowledge of birth control methods by educated females but also due to the late marriages after education. Generally, the husbands of educated females were also more educated and therefore having more knowledge of methods of birth control and also more desire for family planning to maintain a higher standard of living. The 16th round of the National Sample Survey 1960-61 also showed similar results. The studies by demographers Prof. Mukherji and Driver E.D. have also confirmed differential fertility on different educational levels. This is shown in the table no. 6(1) given below:

## Table No. 6(1) : Average number of children born alive to couples classified by educational level of husband & Wife

| Mukherji R.K. & Singh Baljit* | | | | Driver E.D.** | | | |
|---|---|---|---|---|---|---|---|
| Wife | | Husband | | Wife | | Husband | |
| Illiterate | 3.5 | Illiterate | 3.5 | Illiterate | 4.7 | Illiterate | 5.0 |
| Primary | 3.4 | Primary | 3.3 | Primary | 4.3 | Primary | 4.3 |
| Secondary | 3.1 | Secondary | 3.2 | Above | 3.4 | Middle | 4.1 |
| Technical | 3.0 | Technical | 3.2 | Primary | 4.5 | High | 3.9 |
| College | 3.0 | College | 3.4 | Total | | School | 4.3 |
| Post | 2.5 | Post | 3.3 | | | Intermediat | 3.9 |
| Graduate | 3.7 | Graduate | 4.0 | | | e | 4.5 |
| Private Educ. | | Private Educ. | | | | College | |
| | | | | | | Total | |

Prof. Shakya (1986) has observed that there is an inverse relationship between education attainment and no. of children born per'000 female which is shown in the following table no. 6(2) :***

| Wives' education | No. of wives | Total no. of children | Total no. of children per'000 wives |
|---|---|---|---|
| Illiterate | 729 | 4420 | 6063 |
| Literate | 334 | 1579 | 4727 |
| J.H.S. | 141 | 568 | 4028 |
| High School | 269 | 986 | 3665 |
| Tech. Diploma | 2 | 5 | 2500 |
| Intermediate | 94 | 333 | 3542 |
| Graduate | 192 | 534 | 2781 |
| P.G. & Ph.D. | 66 | 168 | 2545 |
| **Total** | **1827** | **8593** | **4703** |

It is clear from the above table that the average fertility rate per woman is 4.7 among rural women. He also found that "the higher the educational level, the lower is the family size". However, at the highest educational level the curve has shown an upward tendency. It is also found in the same study that educated women marry at a higher age, and they also use more sophisticated methods of birth control and also more often.

In an another study, **Srivastava (2009)**\** found that the most important social factor determining low fertility is education,

***    Shakya L.R. ; Fertility Level and Educational Status- A Case Study of Rural Mainpuri District of U.P., Published Ph.D. thesis, Research Publications (Raj.) Jaipur, 1986, p. 65.

*Srivastava M.K. ; Educational and Fertility; Published article, Bulletin Quarterly, G.G.I. of Rural Health and family welfare, Madurai, Tamil Nadu, Vol. 40 (32), 61-67, 2009.

bringing a rational outlook, knowledge of means of birth control, individual health care, economic ambitions and realization of personal ends. Of these the last is most important. He also observed that fertility among educated women is lower as compared with illiterate women. The percentage of educated women in Hindus is always higher, as compared with Muslim women. Usually the Muslim couples, being poor, want and believe in more children due to the faith in Islam.

The researcher has also studied the fertility behaviour with respect to the educational status of Muslim couple respondents of Shikohabad city. In order to evaluate the nature and extent of fertility in the city, the study has been primarily made on the basis of distribution of Muslim couples. Education, being the main potential determinant of fertility, has been chosen as a basis for stratification and further analysis. Thus on the grounds of seven-fold educational standards, a detailed tabulation has been done to cover various fertility differentials.

**MALE'S EDUCATION AND CHILDREN EVER BORN:**

Here an effort has been made to study the effect of educational status of husband on the number of children ever born:

**Table No. 6(3) : Distribution of respondent males by education and the number of children ever born**

| Male's Education | No. of males | Number of children ever born (frequencies) | | | Number of children ever born per'000 males |
|---|---|---|---|---|---|
| | | Living | Dead | Total | |
| Illiterate | 109 | 654 | 114 | 768 | 7211 |
| Literate | 31 | 174 | 38 | 212 | 6838 |
| Primary & J.H.S. | 62 | 192 | 28 | 220 | 3548 |
| Madhyamic & | 76 | 196 | 30 | 226 | 2973 |
| Inter | 16 | 43 | 03 | 46 | 2875 |
| Graduate | 05 | 09 | 03 | 12 | 2400 |
| Post Graduate Others/Technical | 01 | 02 | 01 | 03 | 3000 |
| **Total** | **300** | **1041** | **217** | **1258** | **4193** |

Table 6(3) shows that 109 illiterate males had 768 children, 31 literate males had 212 children, 62 primary and Junior High School had 220 children, 76 madhyamic and Intermediate had 226 children, 16 Graduates had 46 children, 5 post graduates had 12 children and one other/Technical educated male had 3 children.

The per thousand analysis shows that the illiterate males had 7211 children per thousand, literate males had 6838 children per thousand, primary and Junior high school pass males had 3548 children per thousand, madhyamic and intermediate pass males had 2973 children per thousand, Graduate males had 2875 children per thousand, post graduate males had 2400 children per thousand and others/ technically trained had 3000 children per thousand males.

It is clear from the above analysis that the wives of illiterate males had produced the highest number of children; it decreases with the increase in the educational status of husbands. Post Graduate has the lowest number of children. Thus there exists a clear negative relationship between male's education and total number of births of their wives.

The table clearly illustrates the total number of children ever born is not uniformly distributed in the various educational groups of males.

As regards the co-efficient of linear correlation between the educational status of male respondents and the number of children ever born, it was calculated to be (-) 0.94. This shows that there is a high degree of negative co-relation between the educational status of males and the number of children ever born.

## WIVE'S EDUCATION AND CHILDREN EVER BORN:

Under this head, the discussion is concerned with the effect of educational achievement of wives on the number of children ever born. It is hoped that such an analysis will reveal the effect of wives' education on fertility.

The responses relating to total number of children ever born have been computed as a function of educational status of wives.

# Table No. 6(4) : Distribution of wives by education and number of children ever born

| Wives' Education | No. of wives | Number of children ever born (frequencies) | | | Number of children ever born per'000 females |
|---|---|---|---|---|---|
| | | Living | Dead | Total | |
| Illiterate | 182 | 990 | 102 | 1092 | 6000 |
| Literate | 28 | 123 | 19 | 142 | 5071 |
| Primary & J.H.S. | 53 | 207 | 37 | 244 | 4603 |
| Madhyamic & | 25 | 81 | 04 | 85 | 3400 |
| Inter | 07 | 14 | 03 | 17 | 2428 |
| Graduate | 01 | 02 | -- | 02 | 2000 |
| Post Graduate Others/Technical | 04 | 05 | 01 | 06 | 1500 |
| **Total** | **300** | **1422** | **166** | **1588** | **5293** |

Table no. 6(4) shows that 182 illiterate wives had 1092 children, 28 literate wives had 142 children, 53 primary and Junior high school wives had 244 children, 25 madhyamic and intermediate wives had 85 children, 7 graduate wives had 17 children while one post graduate wife had 2 children and 5 others/technically trained wives had 6 children ever born.

The per thousand analysis shows that illiterate wives had 6000 children per thousand, literate wives had 5071 children per thousand, primary and junior high school pass wives had 4603 children per thousand, madhyamic and intermediate pass wives had 3400 children per thousand, graduate wives had 2428 children per thousand while post graduate wives had 2000 children per thousand and other/technically trained wives had 1500 children per thousand females.

Thus, it is evident from the analysis of the data of above table that illiterate wives had the highest number of children ever born and the number of children ever born decreases with the increase of educational status of wives and the others/technical diploma/degree holder wives had the lowest number of children ever born.

As such, it is clear from the analysis that there exists a clear negative relationship between the wives' education and the total number of children ever born i.e. as the educational standard of the wife increases, the total number of children ever born decreases.

A more significant fact was observed that the co-efficient of linear correlation between the educational standard of wives and the number of children ever born was of a very high tune because it was computed as (-) 0.98. Again it shows a very high degree of negative correlation among the aforesaid variables.

**MALE'S EDUCATION AND THE COMPLETED SIZE OF FAMILY (BEFORE STUDY):**

Now an effort has been made to study the effect of educational achievements of husbands on total fertility. The findings relating to the completed family size have been computed as a function of educational status of husbands. The following table no. 6(5) shows the distribution of respondent males by education and completed family size:

**Table No. 6(5) : Distribution of respondent males by education and completed family size**

| Male's Education | No. of males | Total number of children | Average family size with couple (approximately) | Total number of children per thousand males |
|---|---|---|---|---|
| Illiterate | 109 | 768 | 9.0 | 7045 |
| Literate | 31 | 212 | 8.8 | 6838 |
| Primary & J.H.S. | 62 | 220 | 5.5 | 3548 |
| Madhyamic & Inter | 76 | 226 | 4.9 | 2973 |
| Graduate | 16 | 46 | 4.8 | 2875 |
| Post Graduate | 05 | 12 | 4.4 | 2400 |
| Others/Technical | 01 | 03 | 5.0 | 3000 |
| **Total** | **300** | **1258** | **6.19** | **4193** |

The table no. 6(5) shows that 300 males who had completed their family size, had 109 illiterate, 31 literate, 62 primary and Junior high school, 76 madhyamic and intermediate, 16 graduates, 5 post graduates and only one other/technical educated.

The above table further illustrates that the average completed family size of illiterates (with children and couples) was 9.0, completed family size of literates was 8.8, average completed family size of primary and junior high school passed was 5.5, madhyamic and intermediate pass males average completed size of family was 4.9, graduate males average completed size of family was 4.8, post graduate males average completed size of family was

4.4 while other/ technically trained males average completed size of family was 5.0.

The per thousand analysis illustrates that illiterate males had total number of children 7045 per thousand, literate males had total number of children 68.3 per thousand, primary and junior high school pass males had total number of children 3548 per thousand, madhyamic and intermediate pass males had total number of children 2973 per thousand, graduate males had total number of children 2875 per thousand, post graduate males had total number of children 2400 per thousand, while others/technically trained males had total number of children 3000 per thousand. The total average number of children (on an average of 300 males had) 4193 per thousand and an average the family size including parents is found 4.19 approximately.

It is evident from the above table no. 6(5) that the illiterate males had the highest average completed family size and the average completed family size decreases with the increase of educational standard of husbands and the post graduate and others/technically trained had the lowest average completed family size.

It is also clear from the analysis that the completed family size is not proportionately distributed in all the educational standards of the males. The co-efficient of correlation between the educational status of husbands and completed family size was derived as (-) 0.97; which shows a high degree of negative correlation between the said variables.

**WIVE'S EDUCATION AND COMPLETED SIZE OF FAMILY:**

Here, the illustration is concerned with the effect of educational achievements of the wives on total fertility. It is hoped that this type of analysis will explain the direct impact to completed family size, have been completed as a function of educational status of wives.

## Table No. 6(6) : Distribution of wives' education and completed size of family

| Wives' Education | No. of wives | Total number of children | Average family size with couple (approximately) | Total number of children per thousand women |
|---|---|---|---|---|
| Illiterate | 182 | 1092 | 8.0 | 6000 |
| Literate | 28 | 142 | 7.1 | 5071 |
| Primary & J.H.S. | 53 | 244 | 6.6 | 4603 |
| Madhyamic & Inter | 25 | 85 | 5.4 | 3400 |
| Graduate | 07 | 17 | 4.4 | 2428 |
| Post Graduate | 01 | 02 | 4.0 | 2000 |
| Others/Technical | 04 | 06 | 3.5 | 1500 |
| **Total** | **300** | **1588** | **7.3** | **5293** |

The table no. 6(6) explains that out of 300 females who had completed their family size had 182 illiterates, 28 literates, 53 primary and junior high school, 25 madhyamic and intermediates, 7 graduates, one post graduate and 4 others/technically trained. The average family size of illiterates was 8.0, family size of literates was 7.1, size of family of primary and junior high school was 6.6, size of family of madhyamic and intermediate was 5.4, size of family of graduate was 4.4, while of post graduates were 4 and others/technically trained was 3.5. It is clear that the illiterate women had the highest average completed family size and the average family size decreases with the increase of educational standard of women.

**CURRENT FAMILY SIZE:**

Under this head, an attempt has been made to find out relationship between the education and current family size. By current family size, we mean the number of living children a couple has with them. To study the current family size of the family according to education, educational standard of the husbands and the educational standards of the wives have been studied:

**MALE'S EDUCATION AND CURRENT SIZE OF THE FAMILY:**

An attempt has been made here to study the effect of educational achievement of the husbands on current size of the family. The responses with regard to current family size have been computed as a function of educational status of husbands.

The foregoing table no. 6(7) reveals that 109 illiterate males have 654 total no. of children, 31 literate males have 174 children, 62 primary and junior high school pass males have 192 children, 76 madyamic and intermediate pass have 196 children, 16 graduates have 43 children; 5 post graduates have 9 children and one other technically trained male have only 2 children.

### Table No. 6(7) : Distribution of respondent males by education and current family size

| Male's Education | No. of males | Total number of children | Average family size with couple (approximately) | Total number of children per thousand males |
|---|---|---|---|---|
| Illiterate | 109 | 654 | 8.0 | 6000 |
| Literate | 31 | 174 | 7.6 | 5612 |
| Primary & J.H.S. | 62 | 192 | 5.1 | 3096 |
| Madhyamic       & | 76 | 196 | 4.6 | 2578 |
| Inter | 16 | 43 | 4.7 | 2687 |
| Graduate | 05 | 09 | 3.8 | 1800 |
| Post Graduate | 01 | 02 | 4.0 | 2000 |
| Others/Technical | | | | |
| **Total** | **300** | **1041** | **5.5** | **3470** |

The above table reveals that illiterate males have current family size 8 (i.e. 6+2), literates males have average current family size 7.6, primary and junior high school pass males have average current family size 5.1, Madhyamic and Inter pass males have average current family size 4.6, Graduate males have average current family size 4.7, post graduate have average current family size 3.8 and others have current family size 4.0

The per thousand analysis show that illiterate males have total number of children 6000 per'000 males, literate males have total number of children 5612 per'000 males, primary and junior high school pass males have total number of children 3096 per'000 males, high school and inter pass males have total number of children 2578 per'000 males, graduate males have total number of children per'000 males, post graduate males have total number of children per'000 males and other males have total no. of children per'000 males.

The above analysis shows that illiterate males have the highest and post graduate males have the lowest average family size. The current family size decreases with the increase of educational status of the husbands.

The co-efficient of linear correlation between educational status of males and the current family size is computed as (-) 0.97, showing a high degree of negative correlation.

## WIVE'S EDUCATION AND CURRENT FAMILY SIZE:

Here, the study is concerned with the effect of educational achievements of the wives on current family size. The responses with regard to the current family size have been computed as a function of educational status of wives.

### Table No. 6(8) : Distribution of wives' education and current family size

| Wives' Education | No. of females | Number of children alive | Average family size with couple (approximately) | Total number of children per thousand wives |
|---|---|---|---|---|
| Illiterate | 182 | 990 | 7.4 | 5439 |
| Literate | 28 | 123 | 6.4 | 4392 |
| Primary & J.H.S. | 53 | 207 | 5.9 | 3905 |
| Madhyamic & Inter | 25 | 81 | 5.2 | 3240 |
| Graduate | 07 | 14 | 4.0 | 2000 |
| Post Graduate | 01 | 02 | 4.0 | 2000 |
| Others/Technical | 04 | 05 | 3.3 | 1250 |
| **Total** | **300** | **1422** | **6.7** | **4740** |

The above table no. 6(8) shows that 182 illiterate wives have 990 alive children, 28 literate wives have 123 alive children, 53 primary and junior high school pass wives have 207 alive children, 25 madhyamic and inter pass wives have 81 alive children, 7 graduate wives have 14 alive children, one post graduate have alive 2 children and other 4 wives have five alive children.

Per'000 analysis shows that illiterate wives have 5439 children per'000, literate wives have 4392 children per'000, primary and J.H.S. pass wives have 3905 children per'000, madhyamic and inter pass wives have 3240 children per'000, graduate and post graduate wives have 2000-2000 children per'000 & others/technically educated wives have 1250 children per'000 women at present. The average children per'000 women is 4740 in current.

It is clear from the above analysis that current family size is 6.7 (on an average), which (the family size) decreases with the increase in the educational status of wives.

The co-efficient of linear correlation between wives' education and their current family size is recorded as (-) 0.96 showing a high degree of negative correlation.

**CHILD-WOMAN RATIO:**

To study the child-woman ratio, the ratio of the total number of children of age below five years to the total number of females in the reproductive age group 15-49 years has been concluded. The information regarding to this was collected from the respondent males, and the data obtained has been classified in two ways. One according to the educational status of husbands, second, is according to the educational status of wives.

**MALE'S AND WOMEN'S EDUCATION AND CHILD WOMAN RATIO:**

An attempt here has been made to study the impact of educational achievements of husbands on child-woman ratio. The responses with regard to child-woman ratio have been computed as a function of educational status of husbands and wives separately. The following table no. 6(9) focuses on Male's and Women's education and child-women ratio respectively:

**Table No. 6(9) : Distribution of respondents (males & females) by Education and Child Woman Ratio**

| S.No. | Male's Education | Child woman ratio | Woman's Education | Child woman ratio |
|-------|------------------|-------------------|-------------------|-------------------|
| 1 | Illiterate | 1.838 | Illiterate | 1.989 |
| 2 | Literate | 1.618 | Literate | 1.758 |
| 3 | Primary & J.H.S. | 1.635 | Primary & J.H.S. | 1.521 |
| 4 | Madhyamic & | 1.545 | Madhyamic & | 1.463 |
| 5 | Inter | 1.365 | Inter | 1.253 |
| 6 | Graduate | 1.272 | Graduate | 1.067 |
| 7 | Post Graduate Others/Technical | 1.217 | Post Graduate Others/Technical | 1.008 |
| | **Average** | **1.498** | **Average** | **1.437** |

In the light of above figures the investigator comes to the conclusion that education has inverse relationship with child-woman ratio i.e. higher is the educational status, lower is the child-woman ratio.

# REFERENCES

1.   Mukherjee R.K. and Singh Baljit; Social Profiles of a Matropolis; Ashia Publishing House, Bombay, 1961, p. 166.

2.   Driver E.D. ; Differential Fertility in Central India, Princeton University Press, New Jersey, U.S.A., 1963, p. 99-101.

3.   Shakya Lalaram; Fertility Level and Educational Status: A case study of Rural Mainpuri, District of U.P., Published Ph.D. thesis, Research Publications (Raj.), Jaipur, 1986, p.65.

4.   Srivastava M.K. ; Education and Fertility, Published Article, Bulletin Quaterly, G.G.I. of Rural Health and Family Welfare, Madurai, Tamil Nadu, Vol. 40, Ank (32), 2009, p. 61-67.

# CHAPTER 7
# Impact of the Family Planning Works on the Fertility of Respondents

The family welfare scheme is a means to achieve social change because it controls the birth rate both in general and in particular as well. Through this scheme, the liability of children and couple towards the society and the notion can be developed among the families. This scheme is concerned with the use of natural and artificial means to control the population growth both directly and indirectly. **Mr. P.K. Batal** in his famous book, "The Population Problem of India" has traced the origin of these family welfare schemes since 1916. In the country like India, the birth rate has to be reduced because from economic point of view as the increasing population nullifies the national output and income growth. From social, economic, cultural, ethical, political, health and hyper-fertility point of view and immediate attention is required to arrest the galloping birth rate, which is now under a declining trend in the last decade. But still its rate of decline has to be regulated according to the economic parameters of the economy. In addition to this education to children, housing, nourishment and other facilities could only be added to the means, if the size of population is kept under reasonable limits through the effective measures of population control. The aim of family welfare is not only to limit the size of family but it includes the functions like consultation regarding age at marriage, fecundity, sex education and marital affairs, which may eradicate family troubles, tensions and difficulties. This scheme includes the programme of prohibition against the killing of female issues and carelessness during the upbringing of children. Similarly, the child care and child bearing of females having physical and mental diseases and disorders are to be given necessary importance.

In such family welfare schemes many religious, ethical and economic difficulties do arise during their implementation. On the religious ground Hindus and especially Muslims, traditionally believe that a populous family is a symbol of prosperity, livelihood and social status. Thus, it was an ethical crime to control the population growth, which is a spontaneous and natural demographic phenomenon of the human life cycle. In this context, abortion is also treated to be an un-natural sin In India. It is believed that the legislation of abortions may lead to sexual corruption among young males and females.

While analyzing the use of various family planning methods, it is important to mention that in the reference year 1985 as many as 109 cases of miscarriage, M.T.P. (medical termination of pregnancy and abortions) have been reported. Out of these still births or fatal deaths some have automatically occurred, while the rest were due to some motivation or any force. As regards the ratio of the aforesaid two varieties of abortions, it was noted that only 18(16.5%) cases of abortions and M.T.P. were got done by the couples on their initiative, while the rest 91(83.5%) reported abortion or miscarriage automatically due to some mispresumption or complication. The above ratio shows that the proportion of motivated and self initiated M.T.P. and abortions is considerable low in this district. This shows that the use of this family planning device is not so popular. This has also shows a backlog in the history of regional fertility.

The family welfare schemes advocates about various direct and indirect methods of population control. Under direct methods, the female contraceptives like Jelly, cream, Paste, Loop, Diaphragm, condom, Copper-T, Tubectomy, Laparoscopy, Oral pills and vaginal foam tablets are suggested. But under the head of male contraceptives various methods like condom, safe period intercourse, interrupted intercourse and vasectomy have popularized. The indirect methods of population control include the education of the couple regarding sex, marriage, parenthood and spacing between children. In this way, the scope of family welfare is more extensive than that of birth control. In fine, family welfare scheme is not only a physical means to check the growth of population but also is a philosophy to construct a healthy and prosperous society.

At the time of survey, the researcher has studied the conditions of adoption of the means of the family welfare among 300 surveyed Muslim couples of Shikohabad city. The following table 7(1) focuses on the distribution of surveyed couples on the basis of adoption:

**Table No. 7(1) : Distribution of surveyed couples on the basis of adoption of the means of the family welfare**

| S.No. | Responses of the respondents | Total no. of couples | Total no. of respondents | % |
|---|---|---|---|---|
| 1 | Yes | 12 | 24 | 04.00 |
| 2 | No | 240 | 480 | 80.00 |
| 3 | Now & then/Neutral | 48 | 96 | 16.00 |
| | **Total** | **300** | **600** | **100.00** |

The table no. 7(1) depicts that amongst 600 respondents, only 12 couples i.e. 24(4%) negligible respondents have accepted that they adopt the means of family welfare, while 480(80%) respondents denied and only 96(16%) respondents replied now and then (neutral). From these figures, it can be analyzed that religion also plays an important role in the adaptability of family planning measures.

The researcher has asked again 'the reasons' to those respondents who did not adopt the measures/means of family welfare. The following table no. 7(2) shows 'the reasons of not to adopt' the measures (means) of family welfare.

**Table No. 7(2) : The reasons responsible for not to adopt the measures of family welfare**

| S. No. | The responsible reasons | Frequencies of respondents | % |
|---|---|---|---|
| 1 | 'Islam' does not allow | 289 | 60.21 |
| 2 | The children become the | 144 | 30.00 |
| 3 | gift of 'Khuda' | 32 | 06.67 |
| 4 | Impose self control | 15 | 03.12 |
| | Not available easily | | |
| | **Total** | **480** | **100.00** |

It is clear from the analysis of the data of above table no. 7(2) that amongst the 480 respondents who did not adopt the measures of family welfare; 289(60.21%) respondents have opined that 'Islam' does not allow, 144(30%) respondents have opined 'the children become the gift of 'Khuda/Allah', 32(6.67%) have opined that they imposed self control and only 15(3.12%) respondents have replied that the means of family welfare are not available easily.

The following table no. 7(3) focuses on the various means of family welfare devices, which are used by the 12 couples i.e. 24 respondents:

**Table No. 7(3) : The distribution of user respondents on the basis of 'the means of family welfare'/contraceptives**

| S. No. | Various means of family welfare devices used by respondents/ contraceptives | No. of respondents | % (with 24) |
|---|---|---|---|
| 1 | Cram & Jelly / Paste | 02 | 08.33 |
| 2 | Oral Pills (Mala N, Mala D, | 03 | 12.50 |
| 3 | Saheli etc.) | 02 | 08.33 |
| 4 | Vaginal foam tablets | 01 | 04.17 |
| 5 | Loop & diaphragm | 11 | 45.83 |
| 6 | Condom | 01 | 04.17 |
| 7 | Copper-T | 01 | 04.17 |
| 8 | Tubectomy, Laparoscopy Sterilization of males | 03 | 12.50 |
| | **Total** | **24** | **100.00** |

The table no. 7(3) depicts that in males the devices and the use of condom is most favorite contraceptive because of its easy availability and use. In females the applications of oral pills, cream, paste and jelly, foam tablets, loop and copper-T are common 4.17% users are reported sterilized either through Laparoscopy, tubectomy and vasectomy. Some of the educated respondents of the sample are found believing in 'safe period' and 'incomplete' intercourse. But in most of the cases, it was found that a large number of couples could not explain the 'safe period'. In this micro empirical sociological study, it is found that 90.21% respondents do believe and blind faith in 'the preaching's of Islam', and follow blindly. Remaining 9.79% (negligible) Muslims who are well educated, believe in family welfare devices. It is noteworthy that the proportion of sterilization among Muslim couples is found almost negligible.

The condition, under which any couple gets sterilized, plays an important role in determining the popularity of sterilization campaign among the public. The following table 7(4) explains the conditions of sterilization:

**Table No. 7(4) : Distribution of sterilized respondent couples by the condition of sterilization**

| S. No. | Conditions of sterilization | No. of respondent couples | Percentage |
|--------|------------------------------|---------------------------|------------|
| 1 | Voluntary | 01 | 50.00 |
| 2 | Motivation | 01 | 50.00 |
| 3 | Compulsion | -- | 00.00 |
| | **Total** | **02** | **100.00** |

It is evident from the above table 7(4) that out of 2 sterilized couples 1(50%) couples have got themselves sterilized voluntarily and remaining 1(50%) couples have their sterilization due to motivation.

**Table No. 7(5) : Distribution of sterilized respondent couples with respect to the number of children**

| S. No. | Number of Issues | No. of sterilized couples | Percentage |
|--------|------------------|---------------------------|------------|
| 1 | After Ist issues | -- | 00.00 |
| 2 | After IInd issues | -- | 00.00 |
| 3 | After IIIrd issues | -- | 00.00 |
| 4 | After IVth issues | -- | 00.00 |
| 5 | After Vth issues | 01 | 50.00 |
| 6 | After VIth issues | 01 | 50.00 |
| | **Total** | **02** | **100.00** |

From the fertility potential point of view, it is necessary to observe the impact of sterilization and its stage of effective operation. The above table no. 7(5) shows that among the Muslim couples in Shikohabad town one i.e. 50% of sterilized couples have got themselves sterilized after fifth issue and 1(50%) have gone to sterilization after sixth issue.

The age at which the couple has got sterilized is significant for the measurement of fertility potential. The following table no. 7(6) shows the age at which the couple has got sterilized:

## Table No. 7(6) : Distribution of sterilized respondent couples by Age of couples

| S. No. | Age of couples (in years) | No. of respondent couples | Percentage |
|--------|---------------------------|---------------------------|------------|
| 1 | Before 30 | -- | 00.00 |
| 2 | 30 – 40 | 01 | 50.00 |
| 3 | 40 & above | 01 | 50.00 |
| | **Total** | **02** | **100.00** |

The above table no. 7(6) shows that 1(50%) couples have got sterilized between the ages of 30 to 40 years. The other 1(50%) surveyed couple have reported sterilization after the age of 40 years and above. It shows that the sterilization has got a normal response in the town.

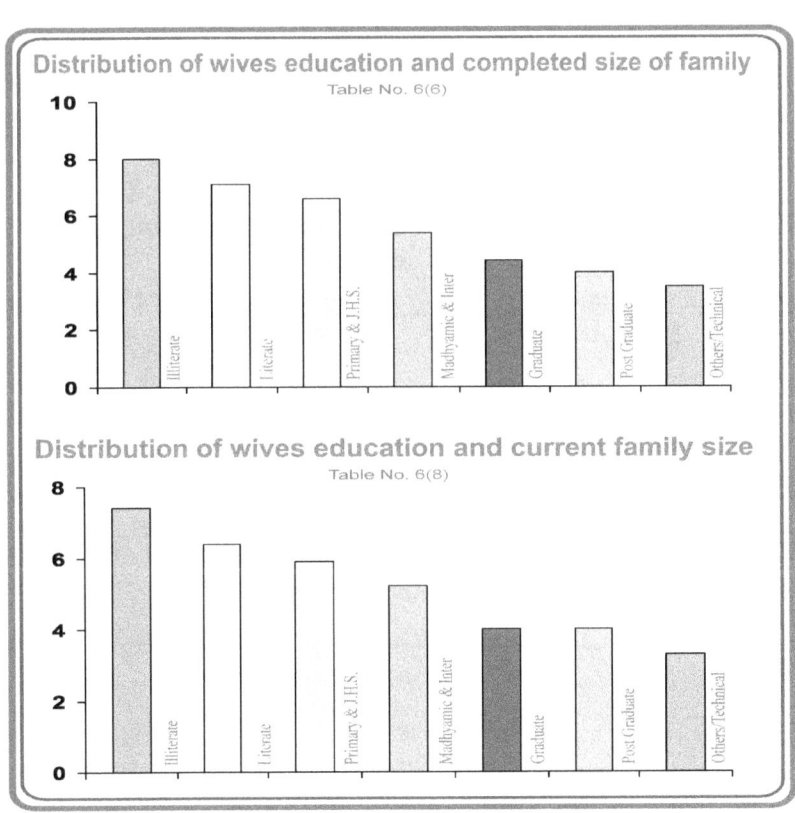

An attempt has been made to evaluate the distribution of sterilized respondent couples on the basis of their annual income in table no. 7(7):

**Table No. 7(7) : Distribution of sterilized respondent couples by their Income**

| S. No. | Annual Income (in Rs.) | No. of respondent couples | Percentage |
|---|---|---|---|
| 1 | Before 6000 | 01 | 50.00 |
| 2 | 6000 – 9000 | -- | 00.00 |
| 3 | 9000 – 12000 | -- | 00.00 |
| 4 | 12000 & above | 01 | 50.00 |
| | **Total** | **02** | **100.00** |

The figures of the above table no. 7(7) shows that in the lower income group Rs. below 6000, 50 percent of couples have reported sterilized while 50 percent couples belong to the income group of Rs. 12000 and above. The following table no. 7(8) focuses on the distribution of respondent couples on the basis of their occupations:

**Table No. 7(8) : Distribution of sterilized respondent couples on the basis of their occupations**

| S. No. | Occupation | No. of sterilized couples | Percentage |
|---|---|---|---|
| 1 | Agriculture | -- | 00.00 |
| 2 | Labor | -- | 00.00 |
| 3 | Shop keeping | -- | 00.00 |
| 4 | Service | 02 | 100.00 |
| 5 | Other | -- | 00.00 |
| | **Total** | **02** | **100.00** |

It is clear from the above table no. 7(8) that out of 2 sterilized couples both couples (100%) are well educated and service holders.

## Table No. 7(9) : The Main opinion of the respondents regarding the state family welfare facilities

| Grounds of appreciation | No. of respondents | % | Grounds of Criticism | No. of respondents | % |
|---|---|---|---|---|---|
| 1. Qualified Doctor | 02 | 06.67 | 1. Non-availability of | 33 | 12.22 |
| 2. Free medicine | 22 | 73.33 | doctors & Nurses/ANMS | | |
| 3. Surgical & Clinical | 02 | 06.67 | 2. Lack of proper medicines | 50 | 18.52 |
| facilities | 01 | 03.33 | 3. Negligence | 70 | 25.93 |
| 4. Medical care | 03 | 10.00 | 4. Lack of satisfaction | 47 | 17.41 |
| 5. Others | | | 5. Ill attitude | 58 | 21.48 |
| | | | 6. Others | 12 | 04.44 |
| Total no. of couples appreciating welfare facilities | 30 | 100.00 | Total no. of couples criticizing welfare facilities | 270 | 100.00 |
| Total no. of couples giving opinion about welfare facilities | 300 | -- | Total no. of couples giving opinion about welfare facilities | 300 | -- |
| Percentage | 10.00% | -- | Percentage | 90.00% | -- |

During the survey only 300 respondent couples could give their proper and main opinion about the family welfare facilities of the state in the district. After the analysis it was found that out of such couples, only 30 i.e. 10% (negligible) percentage have appreciated the nature and extent of these welfare facilities on various grounds. The popular most ground of appreciation was that of free medicine facilities. It was supported by 22 (73.33%) of such appreciating couples. The other appreciations were not given by any respondent couple.

Contrary to the above, there were 270(90%) couples who have criticized the family welfare facilities of the state in the town and district. The most popular ground of criticism was the lack of proper take care i.e. negligence, 58(21.48%) couples have criticized the ill attitudes of the officials and employees of the clinics and 47(17.41%) couples the lack of satisfaction in their service, 50(18.52%) couple respondents criticized on the basis of lack of medicines, while 33(12.22%) couple respondents have criticized the facilities on the ground of non-availability of doctors, nurses and ANMs at the proper and need of time, while 70 (25.93%) respondent couples have criticized on the basis of negligence.

It can be observed that in Shikohabad town, factors like non-availability of resources, lack of public co-operation, social and religious contradictions and indifferences of government officials and lack of trained workers have hampered the smooth sailing of this scheme. Therefore, these schemes could prove marginally affective in controlling the pressure of population among Muslim community of Shikohabad town.

Some Suggestions for Making Programme a Success:

The population of India especially of Muslims is increasing rapidly as compared with food supplies and if this growth rate is not checked then the population problem could be serious to any extent. **Prof. A.G. Kaul**[1] rather rightly said that, "A reduction in fertility would make the process of modernization a success". Drawing attention to the gravity of the population problem of India, demographer Prof. S. Chandrasekharan[2] said that, "We are in great hurry. We cannot wait for a night. One exposure lasting five minutes leads to a baby and every year India adds one Australia to its population". Therefore, there is the need of making the programme of family planning a success. Some such suggestions are:

(1)    The people should be made conscious about making the programme a success. For this they should be properly educated and needed money and technical knowledge be provided to them.

(2)    Adequate number of doctors, nurses, health visitors, A.N.Ms and other field staff should be commissioned into service. They should be made to feel that they are meeting for a national need and as such they should be supplied.

(3)    Latest material concerned with family planning programme should be supplied free of cost in the communities time to time.

(4)    Mobile vans with contraceptives against births etc should be commissioned into service, particularly in Muslim communities.

(5)    Family planning material should be supplied at cheap rates to make popular in the public.

(6)    The people should be properly educated as to how they can enjoy a sexual life without producing children.

---

[1]Quoted from; Hans Raj, Fundamentals of Demography: Population Studies with Special reference to India, Surjeet Publications, Delhi, 1990, p. 319.

[2]Chandrashekharan S.; Population Policy in India; Family Planning in India, Ibid, p.103.

(7) The people should be made to realize the need and necessity of spacing in the births of the children, both for the sake of health of the children as well as mothers.

(8) Family planning facilities should be provided not only in big hospitals but also in big industries, factories and Mohall's of Muslims.

(9) Some economic and financial benefits should be given to those couples who go in for family planning.

(10) The poor, unhealthy and diseased couples should be discouraged from producing children by the workers of family planning.

(11) Co-operation and assistance of both religious and social reformer communities and leaders should be obtained.

(12) To make the programme of family planning a success especially in Muslims, co-operation of all concerned will have to be sought. 'Medical men and women, nurses and health visitors, demographers, chemists, nutrition experts, sexologists, psychologists, social workers would all have to co-operate in building a satisfactory programme to cover all aspects of the vast field of nation building that must be tackled.

# CHAPTER 8
# Test of Formulated Hypothesis

"A hypothesis states that what we are looking for..... a hypothesis looks forward. It is proposition which can be put to a test to determine its validity. It may seem contrary to, or in accord with common sense. However, it leads to an empirical test. It may prove to be correct or incorrect and significant or non-significant." *

*Goode W.J. & Hatt P.K.; Methods in Social Research, Mc-Graw Hill Book Co., 1956, p. 57*

Under this head, an attempt has been made to testify the formulated hypotheses by various statistical tests, to achieve the goals and objectives of this proposed empirical sociological study, logically. The formulae which will be used in calculations are given in chapter no. 2 with symbols. The calculations of the concerning hypotheses are given below:

$H_1$:     "The fertility rate among the Muslims is higher than the Hindus."

This hypothesis is found true and significant in this micro-empirical study. Even then, the researcher has tried to testify the above hypothesis by the statistical test "Coefficient of variance/skewness" (Q). For the calculation, a question was asked to all the 300 respondent couples "Do you agree that the fertility rate among the Muslims is higher than the Hindus?" The responses given by the respondent couples are shown in the following table:

## Table No. 8(H₁) : Calculation of the coefficient of skewness/variance 'Q'

| S. No. | Responses of the respondent couples | Frequencies of the respondents | | Total |
|--------|-------------------------------------|-------------|-------|-------|
|        |                                     | Husbands | Wives | |
| 1 | Yes | 140$_A$ | 100$_B$ | 240 |
| 2 | No | 10$_C$ | 50$_D$ | 60 |
| | Total | 150 | 150 | 300 |

$$\text{Coefficient of skewness (Q)} = \frac{AD - BC}{AD + BC} = \frac{140 \times 50 - 100 \times 10}{140 \times 50 + 100 \times 10}$$

$$= \frac{7000 - 1000}{7000 + 1000} = \frac{6000}{8000} = (+)\,0.75$$

**Conclusion:** The calculative value of coefficient of skewness (Q) is found (+) 0.75, which is positive and very high in comparison to its' standard value and is in between (-) 1 and (+) 1. Hence, the above proposed hypothesis is true and significant.

**H₂:** *"The fertility rate among Muslim women whom have gone through the process of modernization is lower than the one who are traditional."*

This hypothesis is found true and significant in this micro-empirical study [Please see table no. 6(7), 6(8) and table no. 7(1) A]. Even then, the researcher has tried to prove by the calculation of coefficient of skewness 'Q'. The question was asked to all the 300 respondent couples that, "Do you agree that the fertility rate among Muslim women, who have gone through the process of modernization is lower than the one who are traditional?" The responses given by the 300 respondent couples are shown in the following table:

**Table No. 8(H3): Calculation of test of coefficient of skewness 'Q'**

| S. No. | Response of the respondents | Frequencies of the respondents | | Total |
|---|---|---|---|---|
| | | Husbands | Wives | |
| 1 | Yes | 130$_A$ | 90$_B$ | 220 |
| 2 | No | 20$_C$ | 60$_D$ | 80 |
| | Total | 150 | 150 | 300 |

$$\text{Coefficient of skewness (Q)} = \frac{AD - BC}{AD + BC} = \frac{130 \times 60 - 90 \times 20}{130 \times 60 + 90 \times 20}$$

$$= \frac{7800 - 1800}{7800 + 1800} = \frac{6000}{9600} = (+)\,0.625$$

**Conclusion:** The calculative value of the coefficient of variance/ skewness (Q) is found (+) 0.625, which is positive and high in comparison to its' standard value (±) 1. Hence, the proposed hypothesis is true and significant.

H$_3$: *"Fertility behaviour is a function of literacy, poverty and health indicators."*

This hypothesis is also found true and significant in the study, even then the investigator has tried to prove by the statistical test i.e. coefficient of co-relation, which is given below:

## Table No. 8(H₃): Calculation of 'The coefficient of co-relation' (r) by Speerman's rank difference method

| S. No. | Do you agree with the hypothesis (Responses of the couples) | Sexwise frequencies of respondents Husband | Sexwise frequencies of respondents Wives | $R_1$ | $R_2$ | $d=R_1-R_2$ | $d^2$ |
|---|---|---|---|---|---|---|---|
| 1 | 'No' | 10 | 18 | -- | -- | -- | -- |
| 2 | 'Yes' | 140 | 132 | -- | -- | -- | -- |
|  | (a) Fertility behaviour is a function of | 85 | 90 | 1 | 1 | 0 | 0 |
|  | literacy | 30 | 12 | 2 | 3 | (−)1 | 1 |
|  | (b) Fertility behaviour is a function of | 25 | 30 | 3 | 2 | (+)1 | 1 |
|  | poverty |  |  |  |  |  |  |
|  | (c) Fertility behaviour is function of |  |  |  |  |  |  |
|  | health indicators |  |  |  |  |  |  |
|  | Total | 150 | 150 | -- | -- | -- | $\Sigma d^2 = 2$ |

$$\text{Co-efficient of co-relation (r)} = 1 - \frac{6\Sigma d^2}{N(N^2-1)}$$

$$= 1 - \frac{6 \times 2}{3(9-1)}$$

$$= 1 - \frac{12}{24} = 1 - 0.5$$

$$= (+)\, 0.5 \text{ (High and Positive value)}$$

Where   N = Number of terms

d = Differences between ranks

$\Sigma d^2$ = Sum of the squares of

**Conclusion:** The calculative value of the coefficient of co-relation by Spearman's rank difference method, (r) is found (+) 0.5 which is positive and high. Therefore, the proposed hypothesis is true and significant as that, 'the fertility behaviour is a function of literacy, poverty and health indicators'.

$H_4$: *"The aspiration for collegiate education to children would be greater in more modern respondents and their fertility would be lower than the less modern who would aspire, relatively low education to their children."*

The researcher has tried to prove this hypothesis by chi-square ($X^2$) test of significance.

**Table No. 8($H_4$) a: The Calculation of the observatory values of Chi-square ($X^2$)**

| S. No. | Is the aspiration for collegiate education to the children would be greater in more modern respondents and their fertility would be lower than the less modern who would aspire relatively low education to their children | No. of respondents | | Total |
|---|---|---|---|---|
| | | Husbands | Wives | |
| 1 | Yes | 130 | 100 | 230 |
| 2 | No | 20 | 50 | 70 |
| | Total | 150 | 150 | 300 |

Formula: $E = \dfrac{ER \times C}{G.T.}$

$E1 = \dfrac{150 \times 230}{300} = 115$

$E2 = \dfrac{150 \times 70}{300} = 35$

$E3 = \dfrac{150 \times 230}{300} = 115$

$150 \times 70$

$$E4 = \frac{\text{-----------------}}{300} = 35$$

## Table No. 8(H4) b : The Calculation of expected value of Chi-square ($X^2$)

| S. No. | Is the aspiration for collegiate education to the children would be greater in more modern respondents and their fertility would be lower than the less modern who would aspire relatively low education to their children | No. of respondents | | Total |
|---|---|---|---|---|
| | | Husbands | Wives | |
| 1 | Yes | $125_{01}$ | $110_0$ | 235 |
| 2 | No | $25_{03}$ | $2$ $40_{04}$ | 65 |
| | Total | 150 | 150 | 300 |

$$\text{Chi-square } (X^2) = - \frac{(01 - E1)^2}{E_1} - \frac{(02 - E2)^2}{E_2} - \frac{(03 - E3)^2}{E_3} - \frac{(04 - E4)^2}{E_4}$$

$$= - \frac{(125-115)^2}{115} - \frac{(110-35)^2}{35} - \frac{(25-115)^2}{115} - \frac{(40-35)^2}{35}$$

$$= - \frac{(10)^2}{115} - \frac{(75)^2}{35} - \frac{(-90)^2}{115} - \frac{(5)^2}{35}$$

$$= - \frac{100}{115} - \frac{5625}{35} - \frac{8100}{115} - \frac{25}{35}$$

$$= - (0.8695 + 160.7142 + 70.4347 + 0.7142)$$

$$= (-) 232.7326 \text{ (Highly Negative value)}$$

Degree freedom (d.f.) = (m–1) (n–1) = (2 – 1) (2 – 1) = 1

Where m = Row and n = Column

**Conclusion :** Because, the expected value of chi-square ($X^2$) is found (-) 232.7326, which is negative and very high in comparison to the table value of chi-square ($X^2$) (+)3.8415 at d.f. (1). Therefore the proposed hypothesis is true and significant i.e. "The aspiration for collegiate education to the children would be greater in more modern respondents and their fertility would be lower than the less modern who would aspire relatively low education to their children."

**H₅:** *"The more modern respondents who would be better in observing planning tend to have fewer live births, than the less modern respondents likely to observe poor planning."*

This above hypothesis is found true and significant at the time of survey. Even then, the researcher has tried to testify the hypothesis by the statistical test, "coefficient of skewness". For the view point of calculation, a question was asked to all 300 respondent couples, "Do the more modern respondents who would be better in observing planning tend to have fewer live births than the less modern respondents likely to observe poor planning?" The responses given by the 300 respondent couples are shown in the following table:

**Table No. 8(H₅) : Calculation of the coefficient of skewness 'Q'**

| S. No. | Responses of the respondent couples | Frequencies of the respondents | | Total |
|---|---|---|---|---|
| | | Husbands | Wives | |
| 1 | Yes | 115$_A$ | 100$_B$ | 215 |
| 2 | No | 35$_C$ | 50$_D$ | 85 |
| | Total | 150 | 150 | 300 |

$$\text{Coefficient of skewness (Q)} = \frac{AD - BC}{AD + BC} = \frac{115 \times 50 - 100 \times 35}{115 \times 50 + 100 \times 35}$$

$$= \frac{5750 - 3500}{5750 + 3500} = \frac{2250}{9250} = (+) \, 0.2432$$

**Conclusion:** Because on the basis of empirical data, the calculative value of the coefficient of skewness (Q) is found (+) 0.2432, which is in between the standard value of the coefficient of skewness (+) 1 and (-) 1; therefore our proposed hypothesis is true and significant.

$H_6$ : *"The more modern respondents who are more likely to make decisions in the family jointly with wives, would tend to have lower fertility, than the less modern respondents who are more likely to make decisions by themselves ignoring their spouses."*

At the time of field survey, the above hypothesis is found false and non-significant; even then the investigator has tried to test the hypothesis by the statistical test:

Table No. 8($H_6$): Calculation of the coefficient of skewness 'Q'

| S. No. | "Do you feel that the more modern respondents who are more likely to make decisions in the family jointly with wives would tend to have lower fertility than, the less modern respondents who are more likely to make decisions by themselves ignoring their spouses?" | Frequencies of the respondents | | Total |
|---|---|---|---|---|
| | | Husbands | Wives | |
| 1 | Yes | 95$_A$ | 95$_B$ | 190 |
| 2 | No | 55$_C$ | 55$_D$ | 110 |
| | Total | 150 | 150 | 300 |

$$\text{Coefficient of skewness (Q)} = \frac{AD - BC}{AD + BC} = \frac{95 \times 50 - 95 \times 55}{95 \times 50 + 95 \times 55}$$

$$= \frac{5225 - 5225}{5225 + 5225} = \frac{0}{10450} = 0$$

**Conclusion:**  The calculative value of the coefficient of skewness is found zero, which shows that there is no alterability. Therefore, the above proposed hypothesis is false and non-significant.

$H_7$: *"The more modern respondents who are more likely to accord high status to women would tend to have lower fertility than the less modern respondents likely to give low status to women."*

At the time of survey, the above hypothesis is found true and significant [See: table no. 6(6) & 6(8); 5(1) & 5(3) and table no. 7(1) B]. Even then, the researcher has tried to calculate the coefficient of co-relation by Spearman's rank difference method, so that a logical and concrete result may be established.

**Table No. 8(H₇): Calculation of 'The coefficient of co-relation' (r) by Speerman's rank difference method**

| S. No. | Are you agree that "The more modern respondents who are more likely to accord high status to women would tend to have lower fertility than the less modern respondents likely to give low status to women?" | No. of respondents | | $R_1$ | $R_2$ | $d=R_1-R_2$ | $d^2$ |
|---|---|---|---|---|---|---|---|
| | | Husband | Wives | | | | |
| 1 | 'No' | 60 | 68 | -- | -- | -- | -- |
| 2 | 'Yes' | 90 | 82 | -- | -- | -- | -- |
| | (a) an inverse relationship is found between education & fertility | 36 | 30 | 1 | 1 | 0 | 0 |
| | (b) an inverse relationship is found between economic status & fertility | 20 | 25 | 3 | 2 | (+)1 | 1 |
| | (c) an inverse relationship is found between age at marriage & fertility | 27 | 17 | 2 | 3 | (-)1 | 1 |
| | (d) an inverse relationship regarding fertility is found between modern family & traditional | 07 | 10 | 4 | 4 | 0 | 0 |
| | Total | 150 | 150 | -- | -- | -- | $\Sigma d^2=2$ |

$$\text{Co-efficient of co-relation } (r) = 1 - \frac{6\Sigma d^2}{N(N^2-1)}$$

Where  N = Number of terms

d = Differences between ranks

$\Sigma d^2$ = Sum of the squares of

$$= 1 - \frac{6 \times 2}{4(16-1)}$$

$$= 1 - \frac{12}{60} = 1 - 0.2$$

$$= (+) 0.8 \text{ (High and Positive value)}$$

**Conclusion:**  The calculative value of the coefficient of co-relation is found (+) 0.8, which is positive and very high. Hence, we can say that our proposed hypothesis is true and significant i.e. "The more modern respondents who are more likely to accord high status to women would tend to have lower fertility than the less modern respondents likely to give low status to women."

$H_8$: *"A greater proportion of the more modern than less modern respondents would perceive the current incidence of infant mortality as low when compared with the situation prevailed 5 years ago and the former would tend to have lower fertility than the later."*

The above hypothesis is found true and significant in the present micro empirical sociological study. Even then, the investigator has tried to calculate by 'Chi-square ($X^2$) statistical test', so that the logical conclusion may draw:

### Table No. 8($H_8$) a : The Calculation of the observatory values of Chi-square ($X^2$)

| S. No. | Do you agree that "A greater proportion of the more modern than less modern respondents would perceive the current incidence of infant mortality as low when compared with the situation prevailed 5 years ago; and the former would tend to have lower fertility than the later?" | No. of respondents | | Total |
|---|---|---|---|---|
| | | Husbands | Wives | |
| 1 | Yes | 120 | 100 | 220 |
| 2 | No | 30 | 50 | 80 |
| | Total | 150 | 150 | 300 |

Formula: $E = \dfrac{ER \times C}{G.T.}$

$$E1 = \frac{150 \times 220}{300} = 110$$

$$E2 = \frac{150 \times 80}{300} = 40$$

$$E3 = \frac{150 \times 220}{300} = 110$$

$$E4 = \frac{150 \times 80}{300} = 40$$

## Table No. 8($H_8$) b : Calculation of expected value of Chi-square ($X^2$)

| S. No. | Do you agree that "A greater proportion of the more modern than less modern respondents would perceive the current incidence of infant mortality as low when compared with the situation prevailed 5 years ago; and the former would tend to have lower fertility than the later?" – Responses : | No. of respondents | | Total |
| --- | --- | --- | --- | --- |
| | | Husbands | Wives | |
| 1 | Yes | $134_{01}$ | $130_{02}$ | 264 |
| 2 | No | $16_{03}$ | $20_{04}$ | 36 |
| | Total | 150 | 150 | 300 |

$$\text{Chi-square } (X^2) = -\ \frac{(01-E1)^2}{E_1}\ -\ \frac{(02-E2)^2}{E_2}\ -\ \frac{(03-E3)^2}{E_3}\ -\ \frac{(04-E4)^2}{E_4}$$

$$= -\ \frac{(134-110)^2}{110}\ -\ \frac{(130-40)^2}{40}\ -\ \frac{(16-110)^2}{110}\ -\ \frac{(20-40)^2}{40}$$

$$= -\ \frac{(24)^2}{110}\ -\ \frac{(90)^2}{40}\ -\ \frac{(-94)^2}{110}\ -\ \frac{(-20)^2}{40}$$

$$= -\ \frac{576}{110}\ -\ \frac{8100}{40}\ -\ \frac{8836}{110}\ -\ \frac{400}{40}$$

$$= - (5.2363 + 0.0016 + 80.3272 + 10)$$

$$= (-) 95.5651 \text{ (Highly Negative value)}$$

Degree freedom (d.f.) = (m–1) (n–1) = (2 – 1) (2 – 1) = 1
Where m = Row & n = Column

**Conclusion:** Because the expected value of chi-square ($X^2$), is found (-) 95.5651, which is negative and very high in comparison to the table value of chi-square (+) 3.8415 at d.f. (1). Therefore the proposed hypothesis is true and significant i.e. "A greater proportion of the more modern than the less modern respondents would perceive the current incidence of infant mortality as low when compared with the situation prevailed 5 years ago, and the former would tend to have lower fertility than the later."

$H_9$:   *"A greater proportion of the more modern respondents would effectively plan the timing of birth of their children compared to the less modern respondents."*

At the time of field survey the proposed hypothesis is found true and significant. Even then, the researcher has tried to testify the hypothesis by the statistical test "Coefficient of co-relation (r)". For the view point of calculation, a question was asked to all 300 respondent couples, "Do you agree that a greater proportion of the more modern respondents would effectively plan the time of birth of their children compared to the less modern respondents?" The responses given by the respondents are shown in the following table:

## Table No. 8($H_9$) : Calculation of 'The coefficient of co-relation' (r) by Speerman's rank difference method

| S. No. | Do you agree that a greater proportion of the more modern respondents would effectively plan the timing of birth of their children compared to the less modern respondents?" | No. of respondents | | $R_1$ | $R_2$ | $d=R_1-R_2$ | $d^2$ |
|---|---|---|---|---|---|---|---|
| | | Husbands | Wives | | | | |
| 1 | 'No' | 15 | 50 | -- | -- | -- | -- |
| 2 | 'Yes' | 135 | 100 | -- | -- | -- | -- |
| | (a) more modern respondents know well regarding the fertility behaviour | 70 | 32 | 1 | 2 | (-)1 | 1 |
| | (b) more modern respondents know regarding the family welfare schemes | 40 | 50 | 2 | 1 | (+)1 | 1 |
| | (c) more modern respondents become well known with the gap of children | 25 | 18 | 3 | 3 | 0 | 0 |
| | Total | 150 | 150 | .. | .. | .. | $\Sigma d^2 = 2$ |

$$\text{Co-efficient of co-relation (r)} = 1 - \frac{6\Sigma d^2}{N(N^2-1)}$$

$$= 1 - \frac{6 \times 2}{3(9-1)}$$

$$= 1 - \frac{6 \times 2}{3 \times 8}$$

$$= 1 - \frac{1}{2} = 1 - 0.5$$

$$= (+)\ 0.5 \text{ (Positive co-relation)}$$

**Conclusion:** The calculative value of the coefficient of co-relation is found (+) 0.5, which is positive and high. Hence, we can say that our proposed hypothesis is true and significant.

$H_{10}$: *"The percentage of adopters of contraceptives would be higher in the more modern group as compared to the less modern group."*

This hypothesis is found true and significant under this micro empirical sociological study [See table no. 7(1), 7(3), 7(4), 7(8) and 7(9)]. Even then, the researcher has tried to justify by the statistical test 'co-efficient of skewness/variance (Q)'. To calculate the value of coefficient of skewness, a question was asked to all 300 respondent couples, "Do you agree, that the percentage of adopters of contraceptives would be higher in the more modern group as compared to the less modern group?" The responses given by the respondent couples are shown in the following table:

**Table No. 8($H_{10}$) : Calculation of the coefficient of skewness 'Q'**

| S. No. | Responses of the respondents | Frequencies of the respondents | | Total |
|--------|------------------------------|------------------|-------------|-------|
| | | *Husbands* | *Wives* | |
| 1 | Yes | 135$_A$ | 102$_B$ | 237 |
| 2 | No | 15$_C$ | 48$_D$ | 63 |
| | **Total** | **150** | **150** | **300** |

$$\text{Coefficient of skewness (Q)} = \frac{AD - BC}{AD + BC} = \frac{135 \times 48 - 102 \times 15}{135 \times 48 + 102 \times 15}$$

$$= \frac{6480 - 1530}{6480 + 1530} = \frac{4950}{8010} = (+) 0.6179$$

**Conclusion:** The calculative value of coefficient of skewness (Q) is found (+) 0.6179; which is positive and very high in comparison to its' standard value ($\pm$) 1. Hence, the above proposed hypothesis is proved true and significant.

The following table no. 8(11) focuses on the tests of significance of hypotheses and their results at a glance:

## Table No. 8(11) : Test of Significance of hypotheses and their results; At a glance

| S. No. | Formulated hypotheses for the study | The statistical test which is used in calculation | Conclusion of the test |
|---|---|---|---|
| 1 | $H_1$: "The fertility rate among the Muslims is higher than the Hindus." | Co-efficient of skewness (Q) | The hypothesis is found true and significant |
| 2 | $H_2$: "The fertility rate among Muslim women whom have gone through the process of modernization is lower than the one who are traditional." | Co-efficient of skewness (Q) | The hypothesis is found true and significant |
| 3 | $H_3$: "Fertility behaviour is a function of literacy, poverty and health indicators." | Co-efficient of co-relation (r) | The hypothesis is found true and significant |
| 4 | $H_4$: "The aspiration for collegiate education to children would be greater is more modern respondents and their fertility would be lower than the less modern who would aspire relatively low education to their children." | Chi-square $(X^2)$ test | The hypothesis is found true and significant |
| 5 | $H_5$: "The more modern respondents who would be better in observing planning tend to have fewer live births, than the less modern respondents likely to observe poor planning." | Co-efficient of skewness (Q) | The hypothesis is found true and significant |
| 6 | $H_6$ : "The more modern respondents who are more likely to make decisions in the family jointly with wives, would tend to have lower fertility, than the less modern respondents who are more likely to make decisions by themselves ignoring their spouses." | Co-efficient of skewness (Q) | The hypothesis is found false and non-significant |

| 7 | H$_7$: "The more modern respondents who are more likely to accord high status to women would tend to have lower fertility than the less modern respondents likely to give low status to women." | Chi-square (X$^2$) test | The hypothesis is found true and significant |
|---|---|---|---|
| 8 | H$_8$: "A greater proportion of the more modern than less modern respondents would perceive the current incidence of infant mortality as low when compared with the situation prevailed 5 years ago; and the former would tend to have lower fertility than the later." | Chi-square (X$^2$) test | The hypothesis is found true and significant |
| 9 | H$_9$: "A greater proportion of the more modern respondents would effectively plan the timing of birth of their children compared to the less modern respondents." | Co-efficient of co-relation (r) | The hypothesis is found true and significant |
| 10 | H$_{10}$: "The percentage of adopters of contraceptives would be higher in the more modern group as compared to the less modern group." | Co-efficient of skewness (Q) | The hypothesis is found true and significant |

Except hypothesis no. 6, all the above mentioned hypotheses are accepted as principle, because all of these hypotheses (except hypothesis no. 6) are found true and significant in the empirical study and by the tests of significance i.e. statistically.

# CHAPTER 9
# Conclusion and Suggestions

The present investigation and manuscript 'Doctoral Thesis' is submitted to Dr. Bhim Rao Ambedkar University, Agra in the subject of Sociology on the topic entitled: "Effect of Modernity on Fertility Among Muslim Women of Shikohabad City". The thesis is divided into nine chapters in all including conclusion and suggestions. First chapter deals with Introduction and the Review of Literature. Second chapter: Research Design and Methodology. Third Chapter: Socio-economic and Cultural background of the Respondents. Fourth Chapter: Socio-cultural Factors and Fertility. Fifth Chapter: Economic Factors and Fertility. Sixth Chapter: Educational Status and Fertility Level. Seventh Chapter: Impact of the Family Planning Work's on the Fertility of Respondents. Eighth Chapter: Testing of Formulated Hypotheses and Ninth Chapter deals with Conclusion and Suggestions regarding the investigation.

Most of the pre-scholars have stated that the most populationistic religion is the Islam in India. It is both because it prescribes polygamy and also encourages procreation. According to the Fatwa of Sheikh Abdullah Al-Qualquili, "Marry the affectionate prolific woman, for I shall be proud of you among the nation". The ideal of marriage was procreation. It is interesting to note that Ibn-i-Khaldun (1332-1406 B.C.) was of the opinion that a densely settled population helped to achieve more division of labour, more utilization of resources and ensured military and political security. He, however, also pointed out that the vicious circle of population growth leads to luxurious living which in turn causes economic depression and ultimately de-population. The Muslim tradition recommends marriage with four women at one time and the fifth could always be married by divorcing one of the four at short notice. Therefore, the economically well of section procreated at a high rate. The Muslim population has grown fast in almost every country, including India; due to Islam's encouragement to population growth.

The levels and trends of fertility have been found to be low in modernized than in traditional societies. The Indian society which has been traditional for ages is transforming into modern, since independence. Many changes have been taking place in the social, occupational, and political spheres. Consequently a considerable degree of social mobility is observed in the society. The shift in the life style from traditional to modern is expected to have significant impact on the fertility behaviour of the people, besides its effect on various other aspects of life.

Studies classifying individuals or populations on the scale of modernity confirmed an inverse association between modernity and fertility. There is a general agreement in the Indian context that Muslims have a higher fertility rate than the Hindus. The data on fertility is available at community level and there is a general perception that religion plays a vital role in fertility behaviour. However religious communities are not homogeneous groups. Fertility rate tends to vary across different classes within a community. Hence in this research an attempt has been made to study fertility differentials among different classes within a religious community i.e. fertility differential between Muslim women who are relatively modern in terms of education and economic well being on one hand and those who are relatively traditional on the other.

The study of modernity is the key for understanding the fertility behaviour among women. Two major studies that have dealt extensively with individual modernity are: Harvard Project which was carried out in six developing countries (Smith and Inkeles. 1966) and the comparative study of modernism in Brazil and Mexico (Kahl.1968). The Harvard Project was directed specifically towards the investigation of psychological aspects of modernity. A major finding of the Harvard Project is the coherence of modernity syndrome across cultures suggesting that men everywhere have the same structural mechanisms underlying their socio-psychic functioning despite the enormous variability of the culture content which they embody" (Smith and Inkeles, 1966). Kahl (1968) developed a scale of values that differentiated between modern and traditional men in Brazil and Mexico. The Harvard Project and the study by Kahl are the important beginnings in the search for the 'Syndrome' of individual modernity and in the effort to link modernity to fertility change among women. Research undertaken till date shows that the Syndrome of psychological modernity includes the following traits: (1) Subjective efficacy (2) Openness to new experience and change (3) Valuation of time and punctuality (4) Acceptance of the findings of modern science and medicine (5) Granting women rights and equal treatment (6) Autonomy in the field of traditional kinship obligations and (7) Acceptance of family size limitations.

Micro level studies on modernization and fertility are few in the Indian context. A study by Mon Nag (1982) revealed that certain elements of modernization viz. education of men and women, employment of females in non-familial activity etc. are associated with low fertility, while other elements viz. declining breast feeding, improved health, etc. often cause raise in fertility at least in the short run.

Analyzing Harvard Project data collected in Bihar, Pareek and Kothandapani (1969) found a significant correlation between ideal family size and birth control on one hand and some indices of modernity among women on the other. They found that education, personal modernity, political modernization, overall modernization and lack of fatalism accounted for about 10 percent of the variance in preference for a small family among 1,300 individuals. Khan and Parveen (1977) also observed a significant relationship between family planning adoption status and subjective efficacy as measured by the number of stories reflecting realinie coping mechanisms (RCM). Interviewing 1,865 married women in rural and urban strata of three Indian states, Biswanath Mukherjee (1979) found the three core dimensions of modernity-subjective efficacy, openness to change and propensity to plan are contributing substantially to the prediction of knowledge about the attitude towards family planning as well as favourability towards small family size. All the other micro level studies include a few questions on mass media exposure, possession of modern household articles and husband-wife communication (Mahadevan, 1979; Reddy, 1986).

Thus, even the micro level studies, conducted in India had covered one or two of the dimensions of modernization among Muslim women. Further, they could not predict education and socio-economic status among different classes within the community which will have a direct influence on the variance in total fertility. Also the effect of achievement motivation on fertility behaviour due to modernization has not been examined. Hence, it is proposed to examine in greater detail the "Effect of modernity on fertility among Muslim women". The findings of the present study would be of immense value for promoting small family norm through appropriate communication strategies aimed at manipulating women fertility behaviour. In a committee which is perceived to be less receptive of the efficacies of small family norm.

Modernization involves changes not only in the material culture of society but also in its belief system, values and the ways of life on the whole. It is a process of the transformation of a society from its backward outlook to a forward-looking, progressive and prosperous structural build-up, but modernity is the state of change in the attitudes, while modernization is the process of change.

'Modernity has been defined by a variety of indices, such as level of education, exposure to mass media, urban residence, type of occupation, ownership of modern household items or degree of adherence to religious or cultural traditions. When individuals or populations are classified on a scale of modernity an inverse relationship between modernity and fertility is found (Fawcett, 1970).
Modernity has also been found to be related to birth limitation. The study of Korean family planning behaviour by Chung, Palmore and Lee (1972) showed a sensitive relationship of modern attitudes to contraceptive practice. A study by Coombs and Freedman (1979) examined some of the connecting links between modernization in a developing society, particularly urbanization, increased education for women and preferences for a desired number of children.

Status literarily means position in relation to other. The United Nations viewed status of women in terms of actual control on their lives. According to United Nations (1975) the status of woman in society can be determined by her composite status which can be ascertained from the extent of control that she has over her own life derived from access to knowledge, economic resources and the degree of autonomy enjoyed in the process of decision making and choice at crucial points in her life cycle.

During the past few decades the population growth has virtually nullified the efforts of economic development in India. Therefore, the national aim of growth with stability is becoming difficult to be achieved due to the problem of unmanageable population growth. This growth is a result of high level of fertility rate corresponded by a fast declining rate of mortality. Thus, our aim cannot be obtained unless the growth of population is checked. The only factor which seems important is 'fertility', which is to be controlled, first.

'Modernity' and 'Education' are the two most important factors of fertility because these serve the 'motivation' aspect of family limitation. Education should be of a greater importance as a determining factor with regard to fertility reduction. Action can be taken on this front easily and in the most effective manner. We can achieve better results as far as educating the people of Muslim community is concerned. We cannot urbanize, industrialize, raise the standard of living, break the joint family system, change the educational structure and effectively raise the marriage age in a conceivable short period of time as easily as we can educate our people. Fertility, being associated with the vital event of birth is recognized as the fundamental aspect of population dynamics. In order to observe the fertility behaviour among Muslims of Shikohabad city, the present study is a micro level effort. In this context, various fertility differentials like age, income, sex, religion, education, occupation and age at marriage and family planning programme etc. have been taken into consideration. A survey of 300 married couples of Shikohabad city of Muslim community has been done with the help of a pre-tested interview-schedule and observation technique. Through the analysis of such primary information's and data, an extensive tabulation has been done on micro level.

It is clear from the sample that amongst 300 selected Muslim couples, there are 300(50%) male and 300(50%) female respondents, amongst them 3(1%) couples are below 20 years of age, 10(3.33%) couples 20 to 24 yrs. of age, 28(9.33%) couples 24 to 28 yrs. of age, 52 (17.34%) couples 28 to 32 yrs. of age, 90(30%) couples 32 to 36 yrs. of age, 91(30.33%) couples 36 to 40 yrs. of age, 20(6.67%) couples 40 to 44 yrs. of age and only 6(2%) couples are found above than 44 years of age. The figures depict that all the 300 couples are selected of specific age group i.e. 15 to 49 yrs. of age, from which 120(40%) couples are from unclear families, 163(54.33%) from joint families and remaining 17(5.67%) are from extended families. The average number of family members is found 7.85 i.e. 8 members/family and 5.63 i.e. 6 (approx.) children per surveyed couples. Amongst the 300 Muslim couples 57(19%) couples are living in kachche houses, 28(9.33%) in pakke houses and 215(71.67%) in pakke and kachche houses; 12.33% couples are found satisfied, 25% neutral and 62.67% dissatisfied from their living conditions. Amongst the 300 respondent couples 202(67.34%) are found from General caste category, 40(13.33%) Backward and 58(19.33%) scheduled castes and scheduled tribes categories. The researcher has studied the attitudes of the respondents regarding their married life and found that 50% respondents are satisfied, 35.33% dis-satisfied and 14.67% neutral; while the level of the standard of living of 80% respondents is low, 12% medium and only of the 8% is found high. The researcher has also studied the sex wise educational status of the 300 surveyed couples. Amongst 300 husbands 109(36.33%) are illiterates, 31(10.33%) literates, 62(20.67%) primary and junior high school pass, 76(25.34%) high school and intermediate pass, 16(5.33%) graduates, 5(1.67%) post graduates and only 1(0.33%) others; while amongst 300 wives; 182 (60.67%) wives are illiterates, 28(9.33%) only literates, 53(17.67%) primary and J.H.S. pass, 25(8.33%) high school and intermediate pass, 7(2.34%) graduates, 1(0.33%) post graduates and only 4(1.33%) others. According to the analysis of the food habits of the 600 respondents 518(86.33%) respondents are found vegetarian, while only 82(13.67%) vegetarian and non-vegetarian both. On the question; "being Muslim, why are you vegetarian?" The answer was 'we are poor economically, while the non-vegetarian food becomes costly in comparison to the vegetarian food, we; any how are nourishing and act of bearing the children.' The researcher has also studied the occupations of the surveyed couples' families; amongst the 300 couples' families, 200(66.67%) families are engaged in Agriculture, 52(17.33%) in labour works, 18(6%) in services, 9(3%) in shopkeeping and 21(7%) in other occupations, whose an average monthly income is found Rs. 2201/- per family and expenditure Rs. 2609.33 (average) per family per month. It is clear, that on an average debtness/borrowness is Rs. 167/- per family/month. As per these figures & facts, it can be said that the surveyed Muslim families are poor & hand to mouth, and are living in distress and indebtedness.

To achieve primary data regarding the socio-cultural factors and fertility, the investigator has interviewed 300 respondent Muslim couples in face to face situation and found that : (i) the educated husbands are conscious and aware towards limited family (ii) negative co-relation is found between the educational status and the number of children (iii) the increasing level of education is inversely proportional to the number of the births of the children (iv) the educational status of males is inversely proportional to the average size of the family. In other words, the fertility rate among the women becomes inversely proportional to their educational level (v) early marriages promote and encourage the fertility among women i.e. the age of marriage play an important and significant role in fertility (vi) the specific age at marriage of surveyed couples is found 17 to 23 years. It is suggested that it should be increased by late marriages to control the fertility among the females so that the period of fertile union be decreased.

The investigator has also studied age at marriage, specific age and age difference among the surveyed couples on the basis of sex and caste categories. The findings show that:

(i)     In general castes, the difference in the specific age of marriage in the surveyed couples is found 3.0 years, while in backward castes nil.

(ii)    In scheduled castes and scheduled tribes the difference in the specific age of marriage in the surveyed couples is also found 3.0 years.

(iii)   It is also clear that in scheduled castes and scheduled tribes, the marriages of the boys and girls are made in early age in comparison to the general and backward castes. Hence SCs and STs generate more issues in comparison to the general and backward castes among Muslims.

The investigator has also studied the comparative fertility rates of the couples, who do use of contraceptives against child birth and those who do not. From the analysis of achieved data, it is clear that those women who use the contraceptives against births, the fertility rate is found less than those women who do not use the contraceptives against birth. It is noteworthy that amongst those women who use contraceptives, the average fertility rate is found 2.86 while those women who do not use, their average fertility rate is found 4.17.

It is not certain that after married, both the husband and wife will always have cordial relations. There can be and usually are un-healthy and strained relations as well, which result either in separation or Talaq. But Talaq and separation both always does not mean low fertility. It is related to many factors i.e. how frequent is the separation, how much is the separation period, the age of the children, when the parents opt the separation or Talaq, the age of the parents themselves at the time of separation or Talaq, the interval between the separation and remarriage. It is seen that the length of separation and Talaq is more, then fertility will be less i.e. the length of separation and Talaq is always inversely proportional to the fertility. But: (i) those couples; who have the tendency to live together, have more fertility in comparison to those couples who live generally together. (ii) Those couples, who live together whenever, have less fertility. The investigator has found in his study that the fertility rate decreases in the conditions of separation and divorce/Talaq. It is also found that the child marriages & widow re-marriages increase in fertility; therefore these traditions should be restricted because the period of widowhood decreases the fertility. Another result is found that majority of the Muslim couples want and has the desire of more and more issues because of the massage of 'Prophet Mohammad[S.A.W], the angel of Islam, "Do increase in lineage as you can".

Amongst 600 Muslim respondents, regarding the factors which can reduce fertility, 380 (63.33%) respondents have opined in the favour of late marriages, 450(75%) have opined in the favour of restrictions on early and child marriages, 392(65.33%) have opined in the favour of the post partum abistences, 405(67.50%) have opined in the favour of the celibacy, 371(61.83%) have opined in the favour of the tradition of dowry, 443(73.83%) have opined in the favour of the least frequencies of coitus, 460(76.67%) have opined in the favour of the use of contraceptives against births, 395(65.83%) have opined in the favour of the mentality regarding small family, 403(67.17%) have opined in the favour of the anti-attitudes of couples towards the births of the children, 370 (61.67%) have opined in the favour of the Talaq, 400(66.67%) have opined in the favour of the restrictions on remarriages, 445(74.17%) have opined in the favour of the polygamy should be restricted, 389(64.83%) have opined in the favour of to generate the proper awareness among the couples and 405(67.50%) respondents have opined that the fertility may be reduced by enhancing the family planning programmes in Muslim communities.

In the light of above discussion, it may conclude that the factors as, late marriages, restrictions on early and child marriages, separation and divorces, restrictions on post partum abistences, celibacy, tradition of dowry, least frequencies of coitus, use of contraceptives against births, mentality of small families, anti-attitudes of couple towards children, lengthy period of Talaq, restrictions on remarriages, restriction on polygamy, proper awareness among the couples and by enhancing the family planning programmes in Muslim communities, the rate of fertility may reduced.

Undoubtedly; it is true that the economic factors affect birth rate and fertility directly or indirectly, in which economic status of family, occupations, food supply and economic pressure, expenditure of family, conditions of employment, chances of employment, source of income, participation of women in the income of family, economic majesty etc. are important and notable factors, which play significant roles.

The researcher has investigated the economic factors of fertility especially educational attainment, economic status, occupations of husbands and wives, economic groups, economic conditions, desire to maintain status etc. and found that there becomes an inverse relationship between educational attainment particularly of woman and the fertility rate. The higher the educational level, the lower is the family size i.e. educational attainment shows a negative co-relationship with fertility. It is because the educated women marry at a higher age and they use more sophisticated methods of birth control and also more often. And also found that fertility rate goes down with higher economic status. Inverse relationship between economic status and fertility has been also observed. On the basis of this micro empirical sociological study the researcher draws some conclusions as under:

(i)     The fertility becomes low in higher income groups' families in comparison to medium and low income groups' families.

(ii)    The rate of fertility becomes low in service holders and businessmen in comparison to agriculturists and labours.

(iii)    The fertility becomes more in housewives in comparison to the occupationists and serving class wives.

(iv)    The shortage of food supply becomes directly proportional to fertility.

(v)    The economic conditions of families become directly linked with fertility.

(vi)    The birth rate of the children in lower income groups becomes high incomparison to the higher income groups.

(vii)    There becomes an inverse relationship between the expenditure and the fertility.

(viii)    The maximum fertility is found in the daily wage labour class, while the minimum fertility in the service holders. In the light of these facts, it may conclude that 'income and fertility becomes inversely proportional to each other'.

'Education' is one of the most important social determinants of fertility because it serves the 'motivation' aspect of family limitation. Education should be of a greater importance as a determining factor with regard to reduction. Action can be taken on this front easily and in the most effective manner. We can achieve better results as far as educating the people is concerned. We can't urbanize, industrialize, raise the standard of living, break the joint family system, change the occupational structure and effectively raise the marriage age in a conceivable short period of time as easily as we can educate our people.

In the present micro study the researcher has found that the most important social factor determining low fertility is education, bringing a rational outlook, knowledge of means of birth control, individually, health care, economic ambitions and realization of personal ends. Of these the last social factor is most important. He also observed that fertility among educated women is lower as compared with illiterate and literate women. The percentage of educated women in Hindus is always higher, as compared with Muslim women. Usually the Muslim couples, being poor; want and believe in more and more children due to the blind faith in Islam.

The family welfare scheme is a means to achieve social change because it controls the birth rate both in general and in particular as well. Through this scheme, the liability of children and couple towards the society and the nation can be developed among the families. This scheme is concerned with the use of natural and artificial means to control the population growth both directly and indirectly. **Mr. P.K. Batal** in his famous book, "The Population Problem of India" has traced the origin of these family welfare schemes since 1916. In the country like India, the birth rate has to be reduced because from economic point of view as the increasing population nullifies the national output and income growth. From social, economic, cultural, ethical, political, health and hyper-fertility point of view an immediate attention is required to arrest the galloping birth rate, which is now under a declining trend in the last decade. But still its rate of decline has to be regulated according to the economic parameters of the economy. In addition to this education to children, housing, nourishment and other facilities could only be added to the means, if the size of population is kept under reasonable limits through the effective measures of population control. The aim of family welfare is not only to limit the size of family but it includes the functions like consultation regarding age at marriage, fecundity, sex education and marital affairs which may eradicate family troubles, tensions and difficulties. This scheme includes the programme of prohibition against the killing of female issues and carelessness during the upbringing of children. Similarly, the childcare and child bearing of females having physical and mental diseases and disorders are to be given necessary importance.

In such family welfare schemes many religious, ethical and economic difficulties do arise during their implementation. On the religious ground Hindus and especially Muslims traditionally believe that a populous family is a symbol of prosperity, livelihood and social status. Thus, it was an ethical crime to control the population growth which is a spontaneous and natural demographic phenomenon of the human life cycle. In this context, abortion is also treated to be an un-natural sin. In India, it is believed that the legislation of abortions may lead to sexual corruption among young males and females.

While analyzing the use of various family planning methods, it is important to mention that in the reference year 1985 as many as 109 cases of miscarriage, M.T.P. (medical termination of pregnancy and abortions) have been reported. Out of these still births or fatal deaths some have automatically occurred, while the rest were due to some motivation or any force. As regards the ratio of the aforesaid two varieties of abortions, it was noted that only 18(16.5%) cases of abortions and M.T.P. were got done by the couples on their initiative, while the rest 91(83.5%) reported abortion or miscarriage automatically due to some mispresumption or complication. The above ratio shows that the proportion of motivated and self initiated M.T.P. and abortions is considerable low in this district. This shows that the use of this family planning device is not so popular. This has also shows a backlog in the history of regional fertility.

The family welfare schemes advocate about various direct and indirect methods of population control. Under direct methods, the female contraceptives like Jelly, cream, Paste, Loop, Diaphragm, condom, Copper-T, Tubectomy, Laparoscopy, Oral pills and vaginal foam tablets are suggested. But under the head of male contraceptives various methods like condom, safe period intercourse, interrupted intercourse and vasectomy have popularized. The indirect methods of population control include the education of the couple regarding sex, marriage, parenthood and spacing between children. In this way, the scope of family welfare is more extensive than that of birth control. In fine, family welfare scheme is not only a physical means to check the growth of population but also is a philosophy to construct a healthy and prosperous society. It is noteworthy that the attitudes of Muslim community are changing in the favour of family planning but slowly.

The researcher, in his micro study found that all the 300 surveyed couples are not in the favour of the adoption of means of the family planning. They opined that (i) our 'Islam' does not allow (ii) the children become the gift of 'khuda' (iii) The massage of our angel 'Prophet Mohammad[S.A.W] is 'do increase in lineage' more & more (iv) Our Islam did not give the sanction of family planning; therefore we are following these points and the massage of 'Khuda/Allah'.

It can be observed that in Shikohabad town factors like non-availability of resources, lack of public co-operation, social and religious contradictions and indifference of government officials and lack of trained workers have hampered the smooth sailing of this scheme. Therefore, these schemes could prove marginally affective in controlling the pressure of population among Muslim community of Shikohabad town.

Some Suggestions for Making Programme a Success :

The population of India especially of Muslims is increasing rapidly as compared with food supplies and if this growth rate is not checked then the population problem could be serious to any extent. **Prof. A.G. Kaul** rather rightly said that, "A reduction in fertility would make the process of modernization a success". Drawing attention to the gravity of the population problem of India Prof. S. Chandrasekhar said that, "We are in great hurry. We cannot wait for a night. One exposure lasting five minutes leads to a baby and every year India adds one Australia to its population". Therefore in the light of these statements, there is the need of making the programme of family planning a success. Some such suggestions are:

(13)   The people should be made conscious about making the programme a success. For this they should be properly educated and needed money and technical knowledge be provided to them.

(14)   Adequate number of doctors, nurses, health visitors, A.N.M.S., Asha Bahine and other field staff should be more commissioned into service. They should be made to feel that they are meeting a national need and as such they should be supplied.

(15)   Latest material concerned with family planning programme should be supplied free of cost and at the time of need.

(16)   Mobile vans with contraceptives etc should be commissioned into service, particularly in Muslim communities.

(17)   Family planning material should be supplied at cheap rate to make it popular.

(18)   The people should be properly educated as to how they can enjoy a sexual life without producing children.

(19)   The people should be made to realize the need and necessity of spacing in the birth of the children both for the health of the children as well as mothers.

(20)   Family planning facilities should be provided not only in big hospitals but also in big industries, factories and Mohall's of Muslims.

(21)    Some economic and financial benefits should be given to those who go in for family planning.

(22)    The poor, unhealthy and diseased couples should be discouraged from producing children.

(23)    Co-operation and assistance of both religious and social reformers should be obtained.

(24)    To make the programme of family planning a success especially in Muslims, co-operation of all concerned will have to be sought. 'Medical men and women, nurses and health visitors, demographers, chemists, nutrition experts, sexologists, psychologists and social workers would all have to co-operate in building a satisfactory programme to cover all aspects of the vast field that must be tackled.

# SUMMARY

The study of modernity is the key for understanding the fertility behavior among women. Two major studies that have dealt extensively with individual modernity are; Harvard Project which was carried out in six developing countries (Smith and Inkeles. 1966) and the comparative study of modernism in Brazil and Mexico (Kahl.1968). The Harvard Project was directed specifically towards the investigation of psychological aspects of modernity. A major finding of the Harvard Project is the coherence of modernity syndrome across cultures suggesting that men everywhere have the same structural mechanisms underlying their socio-psychic functioning despite the enormous variability of the culture content which they embody" (Smith and Inkeles, 1966). Kahl (1968) developed a scale of values that differentiated between modern and traditional men in Brazil and Mexico. The Harvard Project and the study by Kahl are the important beginnings in the search for the 'Syndrome' of individual modernity and in the effort to link modernity to fertility change among women. Research undertaken till date shows that the Syndrome of psychological modernity includes the following traits: (1) Subjective efficacy (2) Openness to new experience and change (3) Valuation of timing and punctuality (4) Acceptance of the findings of modern science and medicine (5) Granting women rights and equal treatment (6) Autonomy in the field of traditional kinship obligations and (7) Acceptance of family size limitations.

From the study of all factors which directly or indirectly affect fertility, it will be seen that some are really effective, whereas others only very marginally affect birth rate or fertility. In the words of Harrison & Boyce, "The brief survey of direct and indirect factors affecting fertility has shown that for the vast majority of societies there are few social mechanisms for controlling fertility and that those that exist, except in a very few societies, do not appear to be very effective. The fact is that in most societies people do not wish to restrict fertility. On the contrary, they desire to produce the maximum number of children." It is however, difficult to agree with the learned authors that even today the people are not interested in restricting fertility or are in any way interested in having maximum number of children. Today in many societies, the people are quite keen to have limited families and are adopting many measures to check fertility.

In the light of the above discussion, it may be concluded that the factors as, late marriages, restrictions on early and child marriages, separation & divorces, restrictions on post partum abistences, celibacy, tradition of dowry, least frequencies of coitus, use of contraceptives against births, mentality of small families among couples, anti-attitudes of couples towards children, more period of Talaq, restrictions on remarriages, restriction on the polygamy, proper awareness among the couples and by enhancing the family planning programmes in Muslim communities etc. factors may reduce; the rate of fertility may be reduced.

In the light of the data & figures it is concluded that 35 (89.74%) women respondents want limited family and less issues due to, to do proper care of them, to give better education and for the betterment of career of the children/issues. It is further generalized that education has inverse relationship with child-woman ratio i.e. higher is the educational status; lower is the child-woman ratio.

# ABOUT THE AUTHORS

 **Dr. Mudasir Ahmad Qazi** did his schooling from Government Higher Secondary School Dooru in District Anantnag of South Kashmir and B.Sc from GDC Boys Anantnag. He has done B.Ed and M.Ed from the University of Kashmir after which he did his masters in Sociology from Dr. B. R. Ambedkar University [Agra]. He earned a Ph.D in Sociology from the same University. He has got several international publications and attended six seminars and conferences on the themes like Gandhian philosophy, Human rights, women empowerment, population explosion and land grabbing. Presently works as Lecturer School education department, Government of Jammu and Kashmir. Besides he is also designated as approved counselor for IGNOU study centre District Anantnag in Jammu & Kashmir.

**Dr. Atul Kumar Yadav** is the present Head of Department of Sociology; Dr. B. R. Ambedkar University [Agra].